Change Our Hearts

*Faith-Sharing Sessions
for Season Two of*
ARISE Together in Christ

RENEW
INTERNATIONAL

RENEW International
1232 George Street
Plainfield, NJ 07062-1717
www.renewintl.org

Nihil Obstat
Reverend Monsignor James M. Cafone, S.T.D.
Archdiocese of Newark
Censor Librorum

Imprimatur
Most Reverend John J. Myers, J.C.D., D.D.
Archbishop of Newark

Cover design by Robert B. Kelly
Book design by Linda Eberly and Robert B. Kelly

ISBN: 1-930978-62-6

Printed and bound in the United States of America

TABLE OF CONTENTS

ACKNOWLEDGMENTS

We gratefully acknowledge the use of the following quotations:

on pages 11, 20-21, 23, 33, 36, 45, 50, 54, and 60 from the
New Revised Standard Version Bible (containing the Old and New Testaments
with the Apocryphal/Deuterocanonical Books)
Copyright ©1989 by the Division of Christian Education of the National Council
of the Churches of Christ in the U.S.A., and are used by permission.
All rights reserved.

on pages 11, 24, 33, 69, and 78-79, from the *Roman Missal*;
English translation © 1973 International Committee on English in the Liturgy, Inc.
(ICEL)

on pages 13, 26, 62, and 74, from the *United States Catholic Catechism for Adults*,
© 2006 United States Conference of Catholic Bishops, Washington (USCCB), D.C.

on page 28, transcript of talk by Henri Nouwen, first broadcast May 17, 1991
on *30 Good minutes*, a weekly ecumenical and interfaith program on
WTTW11 (PBS) in Chicago.

on page 29, from *The Glory of God and the Transfiguration of Christ*
by A. M. Ramsey, © 1949 Longmans, London.

on pages 41, from the English translation of the *Catechism of the Catholic Church for
the United States of America* Copyright © 1994,
United States Conference of Catholic Bishops—Libreria Editrice Vaticana.
English translation of the *Catechism of the Catholic Church:
Modifications from the Editio Typica* Copyright © 1997,
United States Conference of Catholic Bishops—Libreria Editrice Vaticana.
Used with permission.

on page 44, from the *Rite of Christian Initiation of Adults*;
English translation © 1973 ICEL

on page 51, from the *Rite of Baptism for Children*;
English translation © 1969 ICEL

on page 55, from the footnotes to Jeremiah 31:31ff of the *New American Bible*,
© Oxford University Press, Inc., New York

on page 57, from *Reaching Out: The Three Movements of Spirituality*
by Henri J. M. Nouwen © 1975 Henri J. M. Nouwen, published by Doubleday

on page 59, for the Paco story, based on a report in *The Priest*, June 1999.

on page 59-60 from the article by Barnabas Ahern in *The Critic*, September 1965
© 1965 *The Critic*, published by the Thomas More Association, Chicago.

on pages 63, from *Introduction to Catholic Theology* by Joseph Ratzinger

on pages 63-64, from the *Eucharistic Prayers for Reconciliation*;
English translation © 1975 ICEL

on page 69, from the poem "The Victory" by Thomas Merton in the book of poems
A Man in the Divided Sea, © 1946 New Directions, Norfolk, CT.

Presenting
RENEW International

ARISE Together in Christ is a three-year process of evangelization and spiritual renewal developed by RENEW International. The *ARISE* process is one of the most recent among those that RENEW International offers.

The RENEW process, both parish-based and diocesan-wide, was first developed and implemented in the Archdiocese of Newark, New Jersey. Its success there led other dioceses, in the United States, and in other countries, to bring RENEW to their people and parish communities. In the three decades since its vibrant beginnings, RENEW International has touched the lives of 25 million people in over 150 dioceses in the United States and 23 countries throughout the world.

RENEW International has grown organically from its original single RENEW process. Materials and training have been inculturated and made available in over 40 languages. We have added specific pastoral outreach to campuses, and to young adults in their 20s and 30s. We have incorporated prison ministry, and provided resources for the visually impaired.

The very core of all of these processes remains the same: to help people become better hearers and doers of the Word of God. We do this by encouraging and supporting the formation of small communities who gather prayerfully to reflect on and share the Word of God, to make better connections between faith and life, and to live their faith more concretely in family, work, and community life.

As a not-for-profit organization, our pastoral outreach is sustained in part from the sales of our publications and resources, and the stipends we receive for the services provided to parishes and dioceses. However, our priority is always to serve all parishes who desire to renew their faith and build the Church, regardless of their economic situation. We have been able to fulfill this mission not only in the inner city and rural areas in the United States, but also in the developing world, especially Latin America and Africa, thanks to donations and charitable funding.

As you meet in your small group, we invite you to take a few moments to imagine the great invisible network of others, here in the United States and on the other continents. They gather, as you do, in small Christian communities, around the Word of God present in the Scripture, striving to hear and act upon that Word. Keep them in your prayer: a prayer of thanksgiving for the many graces we have experienced; a prayer that the Spirit will guide all of us so that we become evermore "together in Christ."

This book is gratefully dedicated to
Carolyn and Peter Lynch
and to the Lynch Foundation
for the many ways and years
they have supported RENEW International,
especially the development of
the **ARISE Together in Christ** *process.*

Introduction

Welcome to the second Season of **ARISE Together in Christ**, presented by RENEW International, which takes place during Lent. Each of the faith-sharing sessions has been carefully designed to open us as participants to the rich message that is proclaimed and celebrated on each of the Sundays of Lent and on Passion Sunday. This message is summed up in the Season title "Change Our Hearts."

The Second Vatican Council catches the history, the purpose, and the essential character of Lent in just two words: "baptismal" and "penitential." Behind those words lie whole worlds of meaning, shaped by those who preceded us in faith from the Apostles down to today. When we look to faith share, it begins with the people who are in our groups, but goes beyond that, across time, to those who found the empty tomb, and began celebrating the Resurrection.

Every Sunday is Easter for Christians, because in it we celebrate the Paschal Mystery. In the early Church, one Sunday in the year began to take on a special significance, as the anniversary of the Resurrection. Originally it was only at this celebration (the Easter Vigil) that candidates were initiated into the Church. In the course of this celebration, they were plunged into and rose up out of the waters of baptism, were anointed with chrism, and took part in the Liturgy of the Eucharist for the first time. The liturgical Season we now call Lent evolved from the final and intense preparation for this great feast and new members being born by baptism into the Body of Christ, the Church.

Baptism involves a commitment to a new way of life. The early Church had to face the pastoral problem we still face today: what happens if we renege on our baptismal promises? The Sacrament of Reconciliation was celebrated in a way parallel to baptism, because it was seen as a renewal of baptism. The candidates submitted to a rigorous program of prayer and fasting, to demonstrate their "change of heart" was genuine and sincere. They received absolution at a solemn Mass on Holy Thursday morning, presided by the bishop (the last day on which Mass is celebrated before the Vigil), so that they too could be readmitted to the Liturgy of the Eucharist for the great celebration of the Easter Vigil.

Just as Lent takes its meaning from Easter, so too this Season "Change Our Hearts" takes its meaning from the title of the process, **ARISE**. We cry out for God's help to "change our hearts" precisely because we long to arise together in Christ.

This second Season starts by reflecting on the central call of Ash Wednesday to "conversion," both as "turning away from ..." and as "turning toward ...." Over the next four sessions we explore the meaning of lifelong conversion as radical change. We are guided through these sessions by the great symbolic themes of the Lenten liturgy: being transfigured; from thirst to water; from darkness to light; from Old Covenant written on stone to New Covenant written on our hearts. Our concluding session, in the week before Passion Sunday, leads us into Holy Week with Christ, a week crowned by celebrating the Easter Vigil.

In one of the prefaces for Lent, with which we start the Eucharistic Prayer, we give thanks God for Lent as a
    "joyful season
    when we prepare to celebrate the paschal mystery
    with mind and heart renewed."
That, simply, is the focus and purpose of this Season of **ARISE.**

Faith Sharing in a Small Community

Welcome to the second Season of *ARISE Together in Christ.*

Some of you have already experienced meeting and sharing in small communities. For others, this may be a new experience.

You are coming together as a group, but you are not just meeting together as a discussion or study group where you talk about ideas. Rather, you gather in small Christian communities as a sharing group, open to the Spirit of God, seeking to grow in faith and in your relationship with God, and one another.

For all of you engaging in this spiritual adventure together, here are some key ideas that help bring about good, healthy faith sharing.

Gathering

The first fundamental is that you have chosen to gather as a small community to share prayer, life, and faith in a way that will enrich your own lives, the life of your parish community, and the life of the diocese as a community. The members of the small group need to take the time to get to know one another. Always allow time for introductions at the first session. Then, at later sessions, take a moment or two to ask each other how you are and what has happened since you last met. If anyone new joins the group, again allow time for introductions. The goal is to form a community.

Hospitality and Environment

The right atmosphere is very important for faith sharing. The members of the group need to feel comfortable, physically and psychologically. Effective sharing needs a reflective atmosphere, with as few distractions as possible. It is good to establish a central focus, using something that will help direct thoughts toward the theme of the session. During this Season we explore the meaning of conversion through several of the great symbolic themes offered by the Lenten liturgy. Simple elements can echo and support these. For example, displaying an icon of the Transfiguration for session two; an icon of Christ as High Priest on the cross for session six. A ritual using water is proposed for session three; if practicalities allow, the sharing could take place around a symbolic bowl of water. Creative use of light will enhance session four. For any session it would be extremely appropriate to have a Bible, open at the key passage for the session: this emphasizes the central role that the Word of God has in guiding our sharing.

Timing

It is very important to get the timing of the session right. Under usual circumstances, a session should last 90 minutes. Most groups then extend their time together in a brief social. The time together in the session should have a balance of prayer, talking about our own experience, exploring Scripture, reflection, faith sharing, and talking about ways of living out our faith. This balance is presented in more detail on pages 8-10.

Prayer

Prayer can, and should take different forms. Invite different members of the group to lead the moments of prayer. Do not forget that silence is a very important part of any prayer, so build moments of quiet into the time of prayer, with a gentle but explicit prompt from whoever is leading the prayer. For example:

> Let us spend a few moments in quiet,
> becoming more aware of God's presence …
> … God's presence in each one of us,
> and especially in this community,
> gathered in Jesus' name.

Songs are suggested for the moments of prayer, and all of the songs listed in this book can be found on the *Change Our Hearts CD*. However, these are only suggestions. If you can think of a more appropriate song, then you should substitute that for what we propose.

Experience

Our spiritual lives do not exist without us! Our experience, then, is essential to our spiritual lives. We need to reflect on our story—what we have experienced in our families, in our other relationships—and explore how that relates to the theme of the session. You will notice that the **Breaking Open Our Story** reflections this book offers are usually expressed in the first person. This is not just because they are stories that someone really did share with us. This use of the first person is also designed as a model for sharing, as an explicit encouragement to all of us to dare to say "I remember …" and then to interpret that experience through the eyes of faith.

Scripture

Others before us read their experiences through the eyes of faith, and in it saw the great story of God's loving relationship with his people. This is set out in what we call the Scriptures, the story God reveals to us, most of all through Christ his Son, the eternal Word. The faith-sharing session gives prominence to **Breaking Open God's Story**, exploring Scripture, noticing what word, phrase, or image from it speaks to us. In a word, we share how it has touched our hearts. We are offered input to help us understand what God is saying to us today. Then we reflect together on our experience, our story and God's story—and above all how the two link together. All are invited to reflect: each person who wishes to share his or her reflection aloud is given the opportunity to do so. No one dominates, and no one need talk unless he or she wants to.

Challenge and Commitment

One of the key components of faith sharing is how we take what we hear and share, and live it out in our lives. That is why a moment of challenge is built into every session. We are given the opportunity to respond, not just verbally, but by making a commitment to a clear and specific action that we see as a consequence of living out the faith expressed in the sharing. At the following meeting, we are invited to share how we did at living out that commitment.

We live in a hectic, busy world. Making time for outreach or action will not always be easy. The importance of this moment is the opportunity it gives us to reassess our priorities. The key question is not so much "Did I do what I said I would?" but rather "Through this activity, did I manage to live out my faith?" This should also make us look to the bigger question of living out our faith in the totality of our lives: in our family, in our other relationships, in our work environment. We may discover that rather than doing "more" it might be more important for us to do "less"! This is the time to look at how we are living the values of Jesus and the Gospel, and to identify what needs to change in our behaviors and attitudes.

The Role of the Leader

Each small community will have its leader. In a faith-sharing context, the leader is not someone with all the answers who is there to preach or teach. The leader is a participant, with the particular responsibility of helping the group by

- doing whatever is necessary to prepare for each session. It certainly involves reading over the session in advance, so as to be totally at home with the focus, reflection, and questions. Preparing could also include delegating people to prepare the readings that will be used in the session; delegating the person who will lead the prayer; arranging and/or delegating others to plan and arrange the environment.

- guiding the group through the faith-sharing process. Gently keeping the sharing focused on the theme of the session. Moving the sharing from one moment to another, so that the balance and overall timing is respected.

- listening, and being prepared to ask questions that will keep the faith sharing moving yet focused.

- ensuring that every participant who wants to speak has the opportunity to do so.

More detailed suggestions for the leader are included in *Sowing Seeds: Essentials for Small Community Leaders*, which is part of the **ARISE** Parish Kit (for more details, see page 83).

Faith-Sharing Principles and Guidelines

The following Guidelines will keep your faith-sharing community focused, and help you to grow in faith, hope, and love.

Principles

- Faith is a gift from God. God leads each person on his or her spiritual journey. This happens in the context of the Christian community.
- Christ, the Word made flesh, is the root and foundation of Christian faith. It is because of Christ, and in and through him that we come together to share our faith.
- "Faith sharing" refers to the shared reflections on the action of God in one's life experience as related to Scripture and the faith of the Church.
- Faith sharing is not discussion, problem solving, nor Scripture study. It is an opportunity for an encounter between a person in the concrete circumstances of his or her own life and a loving God, leading to a conversion of heart.
- The entire faith-sharing process is an expression of prayerful reflection.

Guidelines

- Constant attention to respect, honesty, and openness for each person will assist the community's growth.
- Each person shares on the level where he or she feels comfortable.

- Silence is a vital part of the total process. Participants are given time to reflect before any sharing begins, and a period of comfortable silence might occur between sharing by individual participants.
- Before sharing a second time, participants are encouraged to wait until all others who wish to do so have contributed.
- The entire community is responsible for participating and faith sharing.
- Confidentiality, allowing each person to share honestly, is essential.
- The natural culmination of the sharing should be the action commitment, the key to the spiritual growth of both individuals and community.

The Structure and Flow of a Session

On pages 1-5, we presented some of the key elements that should be present for good, healthy faith sharing. We also talked about the importance of a balance. Here is another way of looking at a session, paying attention to the way it should be structured so that there is a natural flow, one part leading the participants to the next, deeper stage.

Having a structured routine frees the group from having to figure out "What do we do next?" It allows the members to concentrate on the what, rather than the how, to pay more attention to their inner selves and to the Word of God.

If you follow the suggested timings, then a session will last 90 minutes.

GATHER (Step 1)   *[15 minutes]*

Elements

- Introductions   *[First time only]*
- Opening Prayer   *[5 minutes]*
- Living Our Faith   *[10 minutes]*
- Focus

Purpose

- This is a sacred time. We enter it deliberately, as a community who have chosen to faith share together.
- We greet each other, we consciously put ourselves in the presence of God and we pray for the grace to grow in faith.

- We share how the previous session has influenced our lives since we last met.
- We focus on the theme of the session that is about to unfold.

[15 minutes]   **BREAKING OPEN OUR STORY (Step 2)**

Elements

- Reflection, based on experience   *[5 minutes]*
- A question, or two   *[10 minutes]*

Purpose

- This part is about "my story," and how it relates to the theme of the session, what it says about my relationships (family, friends, work).
- After listening to a short reflection, everyone has the opportunity—helped by the questions—to reflect upon and share something of their own experience.

[40 minutes]   **BREAKING OPEN GOD'S STORY (Step 3)**

Elements

- Scripture Reading   *[5 minutes]*
- Moment of reflection and brief sharing, prompted by the Scripture Reading   *[5 minutes]*
- A reflection   *[10 minutes]*
- Three questions to prompt sharing   *[20 minutes]*

Purpose

- This part is about exploring "God's story" and in particular how it is speaking to us today.
- The short reflection helps us deepen our understanding of the Scripture text.
- The questions are designed to prompt sharing, which breaks open the Word of God in a way that changes heads, hearts, and hands. Heads: hopefully we may come to a new or deeper understanding of the passage. Hearts: this fresh or renewed understanding prompts a change of attitude on our part. Hands: to what action are we challenged by this?

INVITATION TO ACT (Step 4)   *[20 minutes]*

Elements

- Commitment to an action,
  and suggestions for actions   *[15 minutes]*
- Closing prayer   *[5 minutes]*

Purpose

- This part prompts the participants to understand that faith and faith sharing should impel us to commit to a specific and concrete act in the coming week, which flows from the sharing. This may be either a personal or a group action. Above all, it should be an action that, while challenging, is eminently doable.

- Suggestions, linked to the theme of the reflection, are offered by this book. These are secondary to actions that the group members themselves discern as the fruit of their sharing.

- The faith-sharing session concludes—as it began—in prayer.

"Repent and Believe the Good News!"

> " *Yet even now, says the LORD, return to me with all your heart, with fasting, with weeping, and with mourning; rend your hearts and not your clothing.*
>
> *Return to the LORD, your God, for he is gracious and merciful, slow to anger, and abounding in steadfast love, and relents from punishing.*"
>
> Joel 2:12-13 [NRSV]
> (First reading, Ash Wednesday)

This great season of grace is your gift to your family
to renew us in spirit.
You give us strength to purify our hearts,
to control our desires,
and so to serve you in freedom.
You teach us how to live in this passing world
with our heart set on a world without end.

Preface for Lent II, *Roman Missal*

Focus for this Session

- Conversion is at the core of the Gospel message
- Conversion calls for a change of heart and mind
- Jesus' call to conversion is expressed in relation
  — to God
  — to ourselves
  — and to others
- Conversion is the process of becoming Good News to one another

GATHER

Introductions

Begin this first gathering allowing a few moments for everyone to introduce themselves briefly. Share a little about your life since the end of Season Two. If this is your first gathering share how you became interested in joining the **ARISE Together in Christ** *process.*

Opening Prayer

Leader As we gather for our first meeting
in Season Two of *ARISE Together in Christ*,
let us spend a moment of quiet
in order to become more aware of God's presence...
... God's presence in each of us
and in the community.

One of the members reads the following prayer:

God of compassion and forgiveness,
may everything we do during this gathering
and this Lenten Season
begin with your inspiration,
continue with your help,
and reach perfection under your loving guidance.
We ask this through our Lord Jesus Christ, your Son,
who lives and reigns with you and the Holy Spirit,
one God for ever and ever.

Suggested Song
Change Our Hearts

BREAKING OPEN OUR STORY

Reflection

In Season One of *ARISE Together in Christ*, many of us embarked on an extraordinary journey together, seeking a deeper encounter with Jesus the Christ. Our companions and guides were Mark, Matthew, Luke, John, and Paul. Among other things, we explored how because of our Baptism we are now living a new life, the life of the Risen Christ in the community of the Church.

During this Season of *ARISE*, we will explore the theme of "conversion." Conversion is literally about turning life around; turning away from an old life and turning toward a new life in God. This is founded on the fundamental realization that Baptism is the beginning of a lifelong process of becoming who we already are, the beloved children of God.

For us Catholics, Lent is a privileged time of the year when we are invited to enrich both how we understand and how we live out our baptism. Lent prepares us to journey with Christ into and through what we call the Paschal Mystery (see sidebar): his Passion, Death, and Resurrection, his Ascension, and the sending of the Spirit. In the Catholic tradition, this Lenten journey begins on Ash Wednesday.

The Paschal Mystery

" When we speak of the Paschal Mystery, we refer to Christ's death and Resurrection as one inseparable event. It is a mystery because it is a visible sign of an invisible act of God. It is paschal because it is Christ's passing through death into new life. For us it means we can now die to sin and its domination of our lives, and we pass over into divine life already here on earth and more completely in heaven."

United States Catholic Catechism for Adults, page 93

I have early childhood memories of how much my family loved ashes. I was never happier than when I came out of church on Ash Wednesday with my forehead smeared with that black stuff! On my way to school, my mother reminded me to "take care of the ashes" and not to wash them off, so that everyone knew I had been to church. In fact, as an adult I still get frustrated when the "mark" of the cross does not last all day or is covered by my hair. What makes us such "dirt" lovers?

Unfortunately, there are some people who seem to think that simply receiving ashes is enough. Ashes in themselves have no power at all; they do not make conversion happen in our lives. They are meant to be worn as a sign of a personal commitment to conversion; that I will do whatever I can to turn away from things that damage my relationship with God, with others, and with the natural world; and that I will turn toward whatever helps and fosters those relationships. Ashes should be a tangible, concrete sign—both to ourselves and to others—that we want to live out more fully the life we have through baptism as daughters and sons of God. Whenever we say "baptism" we are saying we belong to the Church: so ashes are in part our acknowledgement that we are in this together.

Sadly, I do not remember being encouraged as I was growing up to have a personal relationship with Christ, and even less to have an understanding of the meaning of conversion. Now, for me, ashes mark the beginning of a privileged moment in the year, and I look forward to taking an honest look at my life and what in it still needs conversion. I am confident I have outgrown my childish understanding of Ash Wednesday. But I wonder if I have truly replaced that with a mature desire for spiritual growth and a solid living of the Gospel ...

Invitation to Share

Take a few moments of silence to reflect on one of the following questions. Then share your reflections.

1. What does having ashes placed on my forehead mean to me?

2. What do you think having ashes on my forehead says about me to other people, both those who share our Catholic faith, and those who do not?

BREAKING OPEN GOD'S STORY

The Word of God

Sometime before the meeting, the leader asks a member of the group to be prepared to proclaim the passage from the Gospel according to Matthew.

Matthew 6:1-6, 16-18
Almsgiving, prayer, and fasting ... in secret

> Reader   The Gospel of the Lord.
>
> **All**   **Praise to you, Lord Jesus Christ.**

Reflect

Moment of silent reflection

• What word, phrase, or image from the Scripture reading touches my heart or speaks to my life?

Invitation to Share

The leader invites those who so wish to echo a key word or phrase that touched them from the Scripture passage.

Reflection

Each year on Ash Wednesday, the Church sets before us the passage we have just heard from the Gospel according to Matthew (6:1-6, 16-18). Jesus' words make it clear that our almsgiving, prayer, and fasting are not to be done to impress others or show them how "holy" we are. Nor is Jesus suggesting we should do good just so that God will love us! Jesus shows us a God who embraces us with love and forgiveness, and our good behavior and penitential practices are our response to God's gift of love. The words we hear as the ashes are placed on our foreheads are an invitation to think of what we are saying by accepting this sign. The *Roman Missal* offers a choice. One is "Turn away from sin and be faithful to the Gospel" (see sidebar on page 16). That is a far cry from a mere display of piety; rather, it is a radical call to conversion and to review our faith and our Christian behavior.

Conversion implies a turning away from something in order to embrace something else; it is the central message of Jesus. Conversion calls for a death and rebirth, a turning away from the darkness to walk in the light, accepting from God the gift of a new mind and a new heart. It is a beginning on which all

The Giving of Ashes

The *Roman Missal* does not specify that our foreheads should be marked by ashes in the form of a cross, but says simply "the priest places ashes on those who come forward."

As this happens, the priest says either

"Turn away from sin and be faithful to the Gospel"

or

"Remember, man, you are dust and to dust you will return."

The first is taken from the first reported words of Jesus in Mark's Gospel (Mark 1:15); the second is from the words spoken to Adam by God in the Genesis account of the fall (Genesis 3:19).

Pope Benedict XVI (Homily for Ash Wednesday, 2007) invites us to see that through the two formulas we should understand it is a rite with a double meaning:

— the first is related to interior change, to conversion, to penance,

— while the second recalls the precarious human condition.

that follows is based, a process that lasts a lifetime. The call to "be faithful to the Gospel" is another way of saying, "God of love, change our hearts and make them one with the heart of Jesus, the Center of the universe!"

Today we read part of the sermon that Matthew includes in his Gospel as a warning against doing good superficially, in order to be seen. We are given three examples: almsgiving (works of charity), prayer, and fasting. All three exist in many religious traditions. Jesus knew them as traditional Jewish customs. We share these three practices, but are invited to interpret and practice them through the eyes of our Christian faith. Jesus contrasts hypocritical or superficial behavior, simply for show, with how disciples are called to live out their faith as Christians.

Almsgiving is now more often referred to as works of charity. In the Jewish tradition, it was part of the Covenant with God: out of love God rescued them when they were outcasts, slaves; an essential part of the response of the People of God is to show the same care for those on the margins (widows, orphans, strangers). For us as Christians, the people of the new Covenant, this takes on an additional meaning, because we are called to see Christ in and to be Christ for the poor, those who are needy in any way. Helping others has been part of the terms of the Covenant with God from the beginning (we will explore the meaning of "Covenant" in session five).

For Christians today, fidelity to the Covenant means to live the Gospel message and to love one another as Christ loved us, without exception. From this perspective, almsgiving is not a sign of righteousness, but a fulfillment of our covenant with God who loves us all equally.

Prayer is the core of who we are. It is what nurtures our relationship with God, and yet it can be so misunderstood. The words of Jesus in today's Scripture strike a chord as much for us today as 2,000 years ago. We must not pray to be seen as the hypocrites do. We do not need to repeat words in order to be heard by God, who knows the deepest truths of our heart.

We can learn a lot from the prayer of Jesus who prayed because he needed to, just as much as he needed food, water, and air. Prayer was his communion with his Father, with his own divinity, with his true identity. In the same way, prayer connects us with God, as adopted daughters and sons with the Spirit of Christ who dwells within us. Prayer also reveals to us who we really are, the Beloved of God.

Often, when life takes us in the wrong direction, we give in or give up. It is all too easy to listen to a culture that promotes *individual*-ism, *ego*-ism, *consumer*-ism, *relativ*-ism, *secular*-ism. Money, power, and competition are some of the gods of our culture and we are tempted to worship them. Lent invites us to turn to what is essentially a happier way of life. We can imagine Jesus telling us, "It is not hard. Come to me and your souls will find rest. Let you heart rest in my heart. Do not worry about words, about how you look, or about your sinfulness. Let go of your need for control and allow me to love you. Trust in my mercy and love."

Fasting, in the religious sense, is the act of willingly abstaining from some or all food, drink, or both, for a period of time. For us Catholics today, one important aspect of fasting has become the custom of giving up something for Lent. In the early Church, it was regarded more like training. Just as anyone today who intends

Entering Lent

" What does 'entering Lent' mean?

It means we enter a season of special commitment in the spiritual battle to oppose the evil present in the world, in each one of us and around us. It means looking evil in the face and being ready to fight its effects and especially its causes …

It means renewing the personal and community decision to face evil together with Christ. The way of the Cross is in fact the only way that leads to the victory of love over hatred, of sharing over selfishness, of peace over violence. Seen in this light, Lent is truly an opportunity for a strong ascetic and spiritual commitment based on Christ's grace."

Benedict XVI
Angelus Message
February 10, 2008

to run in a marathon would watch their diet, run regularly, work out in some way, so too the Christian who is running for the greatest prize of all would use Lent as a special time for preparing to celebrate Easter (see sidebar). Saint Augustine invited his people to understand Lent and Easter as working together: passing from fasting to feasting should help us understand the Paschal Mystery—passing (turning away from) an old way of life to the new life in Christ. So from what should I be fasting? Is it as simple as giving up chocolate, ice cream, movies …? Is that what Jesus meant by "fasting"?

It is far more likely that Jesus had in mind what was already expressed in the Book of Isaiah, which challenges the people of God to see fasting as getting rid of anything that causes injustice and to replace it by sharing: feeding the hungry, housing the homeless, clothing the naked (Isaiah 58:6-10).

If Jesus (and Isaiah) were to re-express this for today, what might they be inviting us to fast from? Would it not be the unhealthy behaviors that do so much damage to our relationships? Our relationships as families, communities, Church, and nations, but also with our environment. Unhealthy behaviors such as violence, envy, gossip, prejudice, hatred, grudges, greediness, and wastefulness. But both Isaiah and Jesus would also say conversion is not just about abandoning these attitudes; it is about positively cultivating the opposite. Ashes are meant to say more about who we want to be than who we regret being in the past.

Invitation to Share

Take a few moments of silence to reflect on the following questions. Then share your reflections.

1. "Prayer reveals to us who we really are: the Beloved of God." What are concrete steps people can take to improve the quality of their prayer? What steps will I take?

2. What are some ways I can better enter into community (that is, share myself with others, with my family, co-workers or parish community)?

3. From what unhealthy attitude, behavior, or action am I called to fast this Lent?

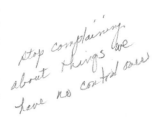

INVITATION TO ACT

Sharing and being together in a small Christian community fosters growth in our faith and in our spirituality. But no communal sharing is complete without a serious commitment to putting our faith into practice.

In this session we have reflected on the three traditional practices that can help us to change our lives and become Good News for the world: to what kind of action does this inspire us?

Some Suggestions

1. Find an opportunity to share of yourself (time, talent, treasure) with someone needy. Do this consciously as a response to the Covenant of love we share as the people of God.

2. Fast from gossiping, violence, criticism, self-pity, or carbon (see sidebar) this week.

A Fast for the 21st Century

In 2008, the Church of England urged people to cut down on carbon, rather than chocolate, for Lent.

They even produced a 40-day plan, listing simple energy-saving actions that can lead toward a lighter carbon footprint, including not using plastic bags, giving the dishwasher a day off, insulating the hot-water tank and checking the house for drafts.

The opening suggestion for Ash Wednesday was to begin the carbon fast by removing one light bulb from a prominent place in the home and live without it for 40 days, as a constant visual reminder during Lent of the need to cut energy. On the final day of the fast, people are encouraged to replace the missing bulb with an energy-saving bulb.

You can download the complete carbon fast suggestions at www.tearfund.org/web-docs/Website/Churches/Carbon%20Fast.pdf

3. Pray for someone who has hurt you. This does not mean condoning their behavior or going back to a harmful relationship.

4. Each year the United States Conference of Catholic Bishops publishes resources for Lent, including selections from relevant Church documents, and guided Scripture reading. Consult the website, and download something that you commit to do each day: www.nccbuscc.org/lent/

Closing Prayer

Suggested Song

Psalm 51: Create in Me

Or recite these verses from the Psalm alternately

Leader   Let us pray together in the words of Psalm 51, a psalm that the Church encourages us to use throughout our Lenten journey.

Side 1   Have mercy on me, O God,
     according to your steadfast love;
according to your abundant mercy
     blot out my transgressions.
Wash me thoroughly from my iniquity,
     and cleanse me from my sin.

Side 2   For I know my transgressions,
     and my sin is ever before me.
Against you, you alone, have I sinned,
     and done what is evil in your sight,

Side 1   Create in me a clean heart, O God,
     and put a new and right spirit within me.
Do not cast me away from your presence,
     and do not take your holy spirit from me.

Side 2   Restore to me the joy of your salvation,
     and sustain in me a willing spirit.
O Lord, open my lips,
     and my mouth will declare your praise.

Psalm 51:1-4a, 10-12, 15 [NRSV]

Leader   In the spirit of the psalm,
           let us offer spontaneous prayers,
           asking God to give us the strength
           to fulfill our Lenten practices,
           that these may truly bring us to a deeper relationship
           with God, with each other, and with our world.

           To each petition, let us respond:

All   **Give us, O Lord, a heart renewed.**

           After the spontaneous prayer:

Leader   Jesus tells us the Father knows already what we need.
           Let us join hands,
           and pray together the prayer
           that Jesus himself taught us:

All   **Our Father, ...**

Looking Ahead

*Prepare for the next faith-sharing meeting by reading
over Session Two.*

In particular:

• *read the **"Focus of this Session"** (on page 23).*

• *read the Gospel passage: **Mark 9:2-10.** It would help
  you set this passage in context if you were to continue
  reading through to verse 13 (verses 11-13 give Jesus'
  conversation with the disciples as they come down
  the mountain).*

God's Beloved

SESSION 2

> *We've got some difficult days ahead.*
> *But it doesn't matter with me now.*
> *I just want to do God's will ..."*
>
> Dr. Martin Luther King Jr.

The glory of God is the human person fully alive;
to be fully alive is to see God.

St Irenaeus of Lyons

> *We did not follow cleverly devised myths when we made known to you the power and coming of our Lord Jesus Christ, but we had been eyewitnesses of his majesty. For he received honor and glory from God the Father when that voice was conveyed to him by the Majestic Glory, saying, 'This is my beloved, with whom I am well pleased.' We ourselves heard this voice from heaven, while we were with him on the holy mountain."*
>
> 2 Peter 1:16-18 [NRSV]

Focus for this Session

- Listening to Jesus, God's Beloved Son
- Being the Beloved of God
- Personal transfiguration
- Facing reality: in life and in faith

GATHER

Introductions

If there are new members to the group since the first session, take a few moments to welcome them, and invite them to introduce themselves.

Opening Prayer

Suggested Song
Who Calls You by Name

Leader   Let us spend a few moments,
becoming more aware of God's presence ...
... God's presence in us and in this community,
gathered in Jesus' name.

Pause for a few moments of quiet.
Then one of the members reads the following prayer:

God our Father,
   in the transfigured glory of Christ your Son,
you strengthen our faith
by confirming the witness of your prophets
and show us the splendor
   of your beloved sons and daughters.
As we listen to the voice of your Son,
help us to become heirs to eternal life with him.
We ask this in the name of Jesus the Lord.

Opening Prayer, Feast of the Transfiguration, Roman Missal

All   **Amen.**

Living Our Faith

Share briefly your experience of putting into effect the action you chose after the last session.

BREAKING OPEN OUR STORY
Reflection

Most of us remember a particular family gathering when all "went well." For me, it happened last year at Christmas. For a change, all of us were able to gather at my daughter's house. Some of the family came by plane; others drove hundreds of miles, and eventually we were all there, happy to be together celebrating the birth of Jesus.

I must admit that I was skeptical. It seems that every one of these gatherings gets spoiled by an inconsequential argument. "You know that I am allergic to nuts, don't you?" "We shouldn't have brought the presents inside the house so soon; now the baby is destroying the wrappings!" etc., etc. In my mind I already pictured my husband getting upset, the children crying, and others complaining about the length of the trip. After a while, just as I was beginning to feel a wonderful period of peace coming to an end, my granddaughter announced that she was going to sing us a song that she had learned in school. "It is about the birth of Baby Jesus," she proudly informed us. The conversations stopped and we all sat in a semi-circle pretending to be in a theater for the big performance.

After everyone quieted down, she started to sing "Away in a Manger." You could have heard a pin drop. There was a reverent silence that could be touched and felt. As we say in some religious circles, "you could hear the angels' wings." Her soft voice and her bright eyes managed to convey in a very simple manner the depth of the celebration. Every time she repeated, "Be near me, Lord Jesus ...," we were transported to the Nativity scene by the sweetness of her voice. It was one of those magical moments ... and, of course, it had to come to an end. After much clapping and affirmation, the children went on with their games and their noise. But somehow something had changed in us; we could sense it in the air. We were avoiding any new conversation for fear of breaking the spell. Yet ... we knew that we had to go back to our sharing and even complaining, hoping that the magic of the moment would last forever.

A Foretaste of the Kingdom

" In the mystery of the Transfiguration, we gain a foretaste of the Kingdom. A hymn of the Byzantine liturgy spells it out for us:

You were transfigured on a mountain.
Your disciples contemplated your glory, Christ God,
so that when they saw you crucified, they would understand
that your passion was freely willed.
They would announce to the world that you are truly the splendor of the Father."

United States Catholic Catechism for Adults,
page 80

In fact, the rest of our time together was wonderful. Although I am not sure we all fully understood what had happened, we were certainly all grateful for the change that was effected by the voice of a five-year-old child who took us to Bethlehem one Christmas Day.

Invitation to Share

Take a few moments of silence to reflect on one of the following questions. Then share your reflections.

1. Share an experience in which you felt that you were taken to another time, another place.

2. Share about how you felt after the experience: about wanting to "freeze" the moment. Why do you think we feel this way?

BREAKING OPEN GOD'S STORY

The Word of God

Sometime before the meeting, the leader asks a member of the group to be prepared to proclaim the passage from the Gospel according to Mark.

Mark 9:2-10

"This is my beloved son. Listen to him."

Reader   *The Gospel of the Lord.*

All   **Praise to you, Lord Jesus Christ.**

Reflect

Moment of silent reflection

• What word, phrase, or image from the Scripture reading touches my heart or speaks to my life?

Invitation to Share

The leader invites those who so wish to echo a key word or phrase that touched them from the Scripture passage.

Reflection

Every year on the second Sunday of Lent, the Church sets before us the Gospel account of the Transfiguration of Jesus (in Year A, from Matthew, in Year B from Mark; and in Year C from Luke). What a contrast between this Gospel and the one we heard about the temptations of Jesus on the First Sunday of Lent! The temptations highlight the humanity of Jesus, who became like us even to the point of being tempted by the devil. The Transfiguration offers the disciples—and us—a glimpse of his divinity. (The first session of Season IV of *ARISE Together in Christ* will focus on the temptations of Christ.)

The text we have just heard today is from the Gospel according to Mark. The scene takes place, we are told, on Mount Tabor, suggesting we should hear an echo of God's appearance to Moses on Mount Sinai (where there was not only the mountain, but also the cloud, and the command to secrecy). Just as God's glory was revealed there to Moses, so now Jesus reveals his glory to three of his followers: Peter, James, and John. The same three disciples will be invited by Jesus to accompany him to pray in Gethsemane—the scene that marks the beginning of Jesus' passion.

Their reaction to what they witness is fascinating. Mark describes Peter as "terrified," and recounts how he seems to want to capture the moment by keeping Jesus, Moses, and Elijah there with them; he asks permission to erect three tents in the hope that

The Life of the Beloved

As a member of a community of people with mental disabilities, I have learned a lot from people with disabilities about what it means to be the beloved. Let me start by telling you that many of the people that I live with hear voices that tell them that they are no good, that they are a problem, that they are a burden, that they are a failure. They hear a voice that keeps saying, "If you want to be loved, you had better prove that you are worth loving. You must show it."

But what I would like to say is that the spiritual life is a life in which you gradually learn to listen to a voice that says something else, that says, "You are the beloved and on you my favor rests."

You are the beloved and on you my favor rests. Jesus heard that voice.

I want you to hear that voice, too. It is a very important voice that says, "You are my beloved son; you are my beloved daughter. I love you with an everlasting love. I have molded you together in the depths of the earth. I have knitted you in your mother's womb. I've written your name in the palm of my hand and I hold you safe in the shade of my embrace. I hold you. You belong to Me and I belong to you. You are safe where I am. Don't be afraid. Trust that you are the beloved. That is who you truly are."

I want you to hear that voice. It is not a very loud voice because it is an intimate voice. It comes from a very deep place. It is soft and gentle. I want you to gradually hear that voice. We both have to hear that voice and to claim for ourselves that that voice speaks the truth, our truth. It tells us who we are. That is where the spiritual life starts—by claiming the voice that calls us the beloved.

Henri Nouwen (1932-1996)
on *30 Good Minutes*,
WTTW 11 (PBS) in Chicago

they could remain in this awesome place until the coming of the kingdom. Jesus shatters their hopes by commanding them to go down the mountain, back to reality. Jesus then instructs them to keep this experience to themselves. This is not the first time Jesus has asked this, but this time he adds "until after the Son of Man had risen from the dead." What they have seen is a foretaste, that will not make sense until after the Resurrection. So, too, our Lent should be lit, even if faintly, by the glow of Easter.

Two very significant figures from the Old Testament appear with Jesus. The presence of Moses and Elijah stand for the Law and the prophets, and beyond that of two promises given by God. The first is the giving of the Covenant (to Moses on Mount Sinai). The second was a promise still not realized, the coming of the "Day of the Lord." We are clearly being invited by Mark to see how the promises of the Old Testament reach their fulfillment in Jesus.

The cloud overshadows not just Jesus, but

the disciples; they are not mere spectators, they are involved, drawn by God into the mystery of Christ's glorification. A voice comes from the cloud: "This is my Son, the Beloved ..." just as the voice was heard saying at Jesus' baptism. But this time the voice adds, "... listen to him." Just as the people of God had to listen to the Covenant entrusted to them through Moses, so now the new people of God must listen to Jesus, who is not just the messenger of the new Covenant, but will himself be the Covenant.

As always, the Gospel invites us not just to observe the disciples, but to imagine ourselves in their place. The first reaction (theirs and ours) is: "Wow, what a magnificent experience we just had on the mountain!" "Why can't we stay here where everything is so transparent and beautiful?" But then comes the challenge: "What will happen to us if we truly 'listen to him'?" "If Jesus is the Beloved Son of God, are we not also God's Beloved?" How this Gospel account ends gives the answer.

The disciples, and then the early community, had to come to terms with the mystery that the new Covenant comes at the price of Jesus' suffering and death—a fate that Peter and James, as martyrs, would share. When Mark's Gospel was first taking shape, the early Christian community was living through persecution and the constant threat of death. To them and to people today who find faith in Jesus difficult, the Transfiguration is offered as a sign of the glory that belongs to the risen Christ, the glorious outcome of the journey through death—not just for Christ but all who are called to arise together in him.

The Transfiguration

The Transfiguration stands as a gateway to the saving events of the gospel, and is a mirror in which the Christian mystery is seen in its unity. Here we perceive that the living and the dead are one in Christ, that the old covenant and the new are inseparable, that the Cross and the glory are of one, that the age to come is already here, that our human nature has a destiny of glory, that in Christ the final word is uttered and in him alone the Father is well pleased. Here the diverse elements in the theology of the New Testament meet.

A. M. Ramsey
The Glory of God and the Transfiguration of Christ

At the same time, this glimpse of glory is set in the Gospel between two predictions of Christ's suffering and death. Being a follower of Christ is not about comfort and external happiness. Those who seriously set out to follow Jesus need to expect that this will demand sacrifice—may even bring persecution and rejection. However, what we see on the mountaintop today can remain with us when we have to come down the mountain to face hard reality. It may be a lot less clear in everyday life, but nevertheless God is with us. Just as in the experience recounted in today's first reflection; long after the little child stopped singing, the peace it brought remained in the hearts of her family.

But perhaps we pass too quickly over the truth that lies at the heart of the Transfiguration, as at Jesus' baptism. It is the twofold message we hear from the voice of God in the cloud.

First, that Jesus is the Beloved Son of God. Baptism and Transfiguration, in Christ, are also ours. We too, are beloved sons and daughters of God. God sees and loves in us what God sees and loves in Christ. Love is our origin; love is our constant calling; love is our fulfillment in heaven. How many of us believe that we are the Beloved of God? It can be so hard in today's society to believe in our "Belovedness" when so many other voices are shouting: "You are no good; you'll never amount to anything; you're too heavy or too skinny; God could never forgive you ..."

Second, we are told to "listen to him." Transfiguration was the overflow of his intimate connection with God, a relationship based on love and nurtured in prayer. This is a relationship that we are invited to share; it began with our Baptism, but it needs to be sustained every day of our lives until it is fulfilled. This is the lifelong process of "conversion" that we began exploring in Session One. What are we moving toward in "conversion"? Our transfiguration! For us, as for Christ, that depends on nurturing our relationship with God as his "Beloved." How? By listening to Christ.

"To listen to him in his Word, contained in Sacred Scripture; to listen to him in the events of our lives, seeking to decipher in them the messages of Providence. Finally to listen to him in our brothers and sisters, especially in the lowly and the poor" (Pope Benedict XVI, Angelus Message, 2nd Sunday of Lent 2006).

Invitation to Share

Take a few moments of silence to reflect on the following questions. Then share your reflections.

1. What prevents people from believing in God's unconditional love for them?

2. What am I afraid of if I come down "the mountain"? Too much work? A change of life? People's expectations of me as a Christian?

3. The voice from the cloud tells us "Listen to him." In what ways, personally and as a community, could we be better listeners to Christ?

INVITATION TO ACT

Sharing and being together in a small Christian community fosters growth in our faith and in our spirituality. But no communal sharing is complete without a serious commitment to putting our faith into practice.

In this session we have reflected on Jesus' Transfiguration and on the reaction of his three friends. God's words echo in our heart: "This is my Beloved Son; listen to him": to what kind of action does this inspire us?

Some Suggestions

1. Pray with the Scriptures 20 minutes each day. You may want to use some of the passages on page 33. When you pray with these or any other readings pay attention to a word that touches your heart. Listen to that word. Let the message both console you, and prompt you to action.

2. Tell someone this week that God loves him or her unconditionally. (For example, as you put your children to bed and say "Goodnight," add simply "God loves you!")

3. We believe that life changes for us with Baptism, when we were marked with the sign of the cross and claimed for Christ. This week, begin and end your day by making the Sign of the Cross, in remembrance of and thanksgiving for your Baptism.

4. Your parish may have candidates who will be baptized, confirmed and receive First Eucharist at the Easter Vigil; pray for them by name as they prepare to make this new beginning in life.

Pray for family + others
troubled times

Listen

Pray

Speak up

Listening to Christ in Scripture

"Come to me, all you that are weary
and carrying heavy burdens,
and I will give you rest.
Take my yoke upon you, and learn from me;
for I am gentle and humble in heart,
and you will find rest for your souls.
For my yoke is easy, and my burden is light."

Matthew 11:28-30 [NRSV]

The Lord is my shepherd, I shall not want.
    He makes me lie down in green pastures;
he leads me beside still waters;
    he restores my soul.
He leads me in right paths
    for his name's sake.
Even though I walk through the darkest valley,
    I fear no evil;
for you are with me;
    your rod and your staff—
    they comfort me.
You prepare a table before me
    in the presence of my enemies;
you anoint my head with oil;
    my cup overflows.
Surely goodness and mercy shall follow me
    all the days of my life,
and I shall dwell in the house of the Lord
    my whole life long.

Psalm 23 [NRSV]

"I am the good shepherd.
I know my own and my own know me,
just as the Father knows me
and I know the Father."

John 10:14-15 [NRSV]

Closing Prayer

Leader Father of light,
in you there is no darkness
but only the fullness of life and truth.
Open our hearts to the voice of your Word
and free us from the original darkness
    that clouds our vision.
Restore our sight that we may look upon
    the glory of your Son
who calls us to conversion and a change of heart.
We ask this trusting in your Word.

All   **Amen.**

(Based on the opening prayer for the Second Sunday of Lent, Roman Missal*)*

Suggested Song

Eye Has Not Seen

Looking Ahead

Prepare for the next faith-sharing meeting by reading over Session Three.

In particular:

• *read the **"Focus of this Session"** (on page 35).*

• *read the Gospel passage: **John 4:5-42***

• *It would help you set this passage in context if you were to begin reading from verse 1 (Jesus passing through Samaria). This is a very dramatic Gospel. This will be more apparent if the proclamation at the next session is in three voices: narrator, the voice of the Samaritan Woman, and the voice of Jesus. Delegate members of the group to prepare the reading in this way.*

• *Water is central to the theme of next week's session. If possible, the faith sharing should take place around a large bowl of water Even if this is not possible for the reflection and sharing, it will be needed for the closing prayer.*

Thirsting for New life

> " At the very dawn of creation
> your Spirit breathed on the waters,
> making them the wellspring of all holiness.
>
> The waters of the great flood,
> you made a sign of the waters of baptism,
> that make an end of sin and a new beginning of goodness.
>
> Through the waters of the Red Sea
> you led Israel out of slavery,
> to be an image of God's holy people,
> set free from sin by baptism.
>
> In the waters of the Jordan
> your Son was baptized by John
> and anointed with the Spirit.
>
> Your Son willed that water and blood
> should flow from his side
> as he hung upon the cross."

From the Blessing of Water at the Easter Vigil, the *Roman Missal*

Water, is taught by thirst.

Emily Dickinson (1955)

Focus for this Session

- Water, symbol of new life in Christ
- An encounter with Christ implies leading others to encounter him
- God thirsts for us

GATHER
Opening Prayer

Leader	Let us spend a few moments in quiet, becoming more aware of God's presence ... ... God's presence in each one of us, but especially in this community, gathered in Jesus' name.

Pause for a few moments of quiet.

Suggested Song

As The Deer Longs (Psalm 42, 43)

or recite these Psalm verses:

Leader	Let us pray together in the words of the Psalms.
Side 1	As a deer longs for flowing streams, so my soul longs for you, O God.
Side 2	My soul thirsts for God, for the living God.
All	**When shall I come and behold the face of God?**
Side 1	O God, you are my God, I seek you, my soul thirsts for you; my flesh faints for you, as in a dry and weary land where there is no water.
Side 2	So I have looked upon you in the sanctuary, beholding your power and glory. Because your steadfast love is better than life, my lips will praise you.
All	**So I will bless you as long as I live; I will lift up my hands and call on your name.**

Psalm 42:1-2 & Psalm 63:1-4 [NRSV]

Living Our Faith

> *Share briefly your experience of putting into effect the action you chose after the last session.*

BREAKING OPEN OUR STORY
Reflection

A few months ago a friend gave us a basket of mangoes as a gift. I had never eaten this fruit and had no idea that I was allergic to it. I must confess that I loved its taste, but hated the effects it had on me. After one day in agony (no need to enter into details), I was so weak that the paramedics had to take me to the hospital. The doctor soon diagnosed that I was having an allergic reaction to mangoes, and warned me I was totally dehydrated. Before going to the hospital, my family had encouraged me to drink a lot of fluids, but I felt so nauseous that even the thought of drinking made me feel worse. After a few hours in the emergency room I was sent home with some medication for nausea.

That night, I fainted in the bathroom because of my dehydration. I cracked my head, and had to be rushed back to the hospital! A simple allergic reaction was the cause of nausea, fainting, and finally several stitches. What surprised me was that although my body was dehydrated I did not feel thirsty.

The same can happen to us spiritually. We can be spiritually dehydrated and not know it; we may not even feel that we are missing anything. We feel down, empty, exhausted, may even suffer from strange headaches, and get sick, without realizing that we are thirsting for God. How often have we felt discouraged and unable to go on in the midst of a crisis, or complained about our life, job, and family? We feel depressed, and then someone helps us realize that actually things are pretty good in our life— simply, somehow we had lost perspective.

Every time I forget that I am the Beloved of God, I become spiritually dehydrated, and it often takes "cracking my head" to remind me of who I truly am.

Invitation to Share

Take a few moments of silence to reflect on one of the following questions. Then share your reflections.

1. Share an experience of "dehydration," of thirsting, of a deep longing for something.

2. Share an experience when someone offered you some words of comfort or quality of presence that helped quench your thirst. What happened?

BREAKING OPEN GOD'S STORY

The Word of God

Sometime before the meeting, the leader invites members of the group to take the following parts in the proclamation of the Gospel: narrator, the voice of the Samaritan woman, and the voice of Jesus.

John 4:5-30, 39-42

"A spring of water gushing up to eternal life."

Reader   *The Gospel of the Lord.*

All   **Praise to you, Lord Jesus Christ.**

Reflect

Moment of silent reflection

• What word, phrase, or image from the Scripture reading touches my heart or speaks to my life?

Invitation to Share

The leader invites those who so wish to echo a key word or phrase that touched them from the Scripture passage.

Reflection

The woman met Jesus at noon. That was a strange time to go to the well to draw water, because the heat was unbearable. Perhaps she went at that time to avoid other women who went in the cool of the morning, and spent a lot of time catching up with the town gossip. When we hear about her lifestyle later, it's easy to imagine she would be the target of that gossip, and perhaps not even welcomed by the other women.

John underlines the fact that this happens in Samaria, and explicitly tells us how Jews did not associate with Samaritans because they regarded them as ritually impure. One key consequence: Jews were forbidden to drink from any vessel Samaritans had handled.

Add to this the fact that a man talking to a woman was a breach of basic religious and social taboo at this time and in this culture!

No wonder the woman was surprised when Jesus not only talks to her, but asks her for a drink! Out of her confusion comes a basic question, to which Jesus gives a gentle reply, full

The "aha" moment of conversion

Throughout the Gospel according to John we are presented with a series of dramatic encounters between Jesus and various characters. To help underline the essential message, these encounters often have a humorous touch.

We see various characters respond to Jesus' message on a first, literal level. This week the Samaritan woman wonders aloud how this man can give her water when he doesn't even have a bucket! Next week we will see Nicodemus asking how he could go back and be born again. But these little jokes of John have a very serious purpose: they keep the conversation going.

It is only as the conversation with Jesus continues that these characters are drawn in deeper, and come to an encounter not just with an interesting man who can make their present life better, but with the Messiah, the Christ, sent to bring them new life.

Watch out for the "aha" moment; it will be a moment of conversion, of turning around, of change …

of promise, speaking of "living water." Her reply shows she is taking this stranger literally: how can he give water without a bucket? Is he talking about some other well? Again Jesus responds, and with each response he is inviting her to a new understanding, to go beyond the literal, beyond what she can see and touch. He explains that this "living water" will become in her a spring welling up to eternal life. For the first time, she does not respond with a question, but accepts the invitation: "Sir, give me this water." A first small step on her process of conversion. And yet, she is still taking Jesus literally, because she speaks of never having to come back to the well.

Why would she not want to come to the well? Not just because of the tedium of drawing water, but because of who she is. Jesus now gently leads her deeper into the process of leaving her old life behind and becoming a new person. The encounter continues to unfold with the questions about her husbands, questions that bring her face-to-face with herself. She timidly shared the truth about her life ... which opens her up to seeing the truth about the person she is now with: he is the Messiah that deep down she is longing will come. John gives us the words of the conversation, but beyond them let us be open to glimpsing the way Jesus accepts her unconditionally, from daring to speak to her in the beginning, to not condemning her for her life-style, at the end of the encounter.

Our thirst for God; God's thirst for us

" She had five husbands and was living with another man. She made ample use of her freedom, but still did not become freer; in fact, she became emptier.

In this woman, we can see the reflection of our lives today with all the problems that involve us; but we also see how, in the depths of our hearts, there is always the question of God. God thirsts for our faith and wants us to find in him the source of our authentic happiness.

Jesus wants to lead us, like the Samaritan woman, to profess our faith in him with strength so that we can then proclaim and witness to our brothers and sisters the joy of encountering him and the marvels that his love works in our lives."

Pope Benedict XVI
Angelus Message, Second Sunday of Lent
(February 24), 2008

We do not know for sure how long this conversation took, but because of the heat and the return of the disciples, it could not have been too long. Yet, it was enough to turn this woman's life around. For however brief a moment, there has been a profound sharing: a sharing of life experience, which leads to faith sharing. Already that is a very profound model for what we are doing in this session. By the end let us hope we, too, will have deepened our understanding, and appreciation of Jesus as the Christ who offers us new life. But the Gospel does not end there! To what action did her faith call her? This sinful Samaritan woman became an evangelizer, telling everyone in the town about Jesus! She could not contain the joy in her heart at having found Jesus, the Messiah. Her sharing, we are told, brought many in the town to believe in Jesus.

The Church has always associated this Gospel passage with the sacrament of Baptism. A special rite, called a scrutiny, takes place on this Sunday for candidates for Baptism at the Easter Vigil (see closing prayer). Baptism makes us members of the Body of Christ; it makes us a new people, disciples of Christ and members of the community of believers we call the Church. When we arise from the waters of Baptism we leave behind our old life as isolated individuals and enter into the new life, as part of the family of God, to become a sister or brother to all. But, as we are discovering consistently throughout this season, being baptized marks more of a beginning than an end. The process of living out our Baptism means converting our old way of life into a new one; it means that we will become not just hearers of the Good News, but bearers of the Good News to others. That is exactly why the word "conversion" has two meanings: what am I doing to "convert" my life; and what are we doing to lead others to "conversion"!

The Gospel story is about thirst: the thirst of the Samaritan woman, and our thirst. But it begins with Jesus' thirst. On Good Friday we will hear again from the Gospel according to John, as Jesus from the cross gasps, "I am thirsty." It is also about the unconditional extent of God's thirsting for us.

God's thirst for us; our thirst for God

" 'If you knew the gift of God!' (John 4:10). The wonder of prayer is revealed beside the well where we come seeking water: there, Christ comes to meet every human being. It is he who first seeks us and asks us for a drink. Jesus thirsts; his asking arises from the depths of God's desire for us. Whether we realize it or not, prayer is the encounter of God's thirst with ours. God thirsts that we may thirst for him."

Catechism of the Catholic Church, 2560

As the preface which goes with this Gospel says: "Christ, in his thirst to receive the woman's faith, awakened in her heart the fire of God's love." It is a mutual thirst, God longing to bring us, in Christ, to new life; us longing for God and new life in Christ. May this Lent sharpen our thirst for God so that we more readily welcome and live out—as individuals and as Church—the new life we have in Christ.

Invitation to Share

Take a few moments of silence to reflect on the following questions. Then share your reflections.

1. Share together on the ways in which the Samaritan woman expresses her conversion (In words? In actions? In both?).

2. Share briefly your experience of moments of spiritual dehydration. Share, too, what helped quench that thirst for God.

3. The Gospel tells us that the disciples are astonished to find Jesus speaking to this woman. Yet this woman proves to be an extremely effective evangelizer, bringing others to an encounter with Christ. How am I open to the surprises that God may put into my life? People that I may meet who help me on my faith journey?

4. If I met Christ at the well, what is the question Christ would ask me, the question that would bring me face-to-face with myself? What are the burdens that I long to be rid of?

INVITATION TO ACT

Sharing and being together in a small Christian community fosters growth in our faith and in our spirituality. But no communal sharing is complete without a serious commitment to putting our faith into practice.

In this session we have reflected on God's thirst for us revealed in the encounter between Jesus and the Samaritan woman. To what kind of action does this inspire us?

Some Suggestions

1. Many people, especially women, in the developing world still have to walk miles everyday for water. Research ways that the group, or perhaps even the entire parish, can help such people. For example, sponsor the gift of a water jug, a water

purifier, a water pump, or even a water truck (see www.oxfamamericaunwrapped.com/product. php?productid=14).

2. The Samaritan woman told everyone about her encounter with Christ. Share your testimony of faith with a family member or co-worker.

3. "Prayer is the encounter of God's thirst with ours" (*Catechism of the Catholic Church*, 2560). In your prayer this week, be more open to what God wants of you, rather than what you want of God.

4. Ask one of the candidates for Baptism at Easter in your parish to share with you what they expect of Baptism. Note their reply, and use it to inform your faith-sharing discussion for the three remaining sessions of Season Two.

Closing Prayer

If possible the faith sharing should have taken place around a bowl of water set in the center of the group. If that was impractical, take time to set it up now. Also have ready small sheets of paper and pens (preferably with water-soluble ink).

Leader	We gather around this water
	as did the Samaritan woman at the well.

We gather around this water
as did the Samaritan woman at the well.
We, too, thirst for living water!
May the Word of the Lord change our lives too,
helping us to come face-to-face
with the sins and weaknesses that burden us.

The leader now invites the participants to write on a piece of paper what it is they long to leave behind, so that their hearts can be more open to God.

If necessary, the leader can prompt with examples, such as: anxiety, fear, envy, cynicism, suspicion …

Explain that each person will then drop their paper into the "well" where it will dissolve.

While the people reflect and write the burden they would like to leave behind, sing or play an appropriate song.

Suggested Songs
The Water I Give

*Conclude with the following prayer,
led by one person, or recited by everyone together:*

God our Father,
keep us from relying too much on ourselves
and never let the powers of evil deceive us.
Free us from the spirit of falsehood
and help us recognize what in our lives needs change
so that, with the help of your Spirit
and our hearts cleansed from sin
we may ourselves advance on the way to salvation,
and bring others with us.
We ask this through Christ the Lord.

All   **Amen.**

Adapted from the Prayer of Exorcism, First Scrutiny,
Rite of Christian Initiation of Adults, 164

Looking Ahead

Prepare for the next faith-sharing meeting by reading over Session Four.

In particular:

- *read the **"Focus of this Session"** (on page 45).*
- *read the Gospel passage: **John 9:1-41**. It may help the group's appreciation of the passage during next week's session to invite three people to be prepared to proclaim it for the next session: one as narrator, one as the voice of Nicodemus, and one as the voice of Christ.*

From Darkness to Light

> **"** The light shines in the darkness,
> and the darkness did not overcome it."
>
> John 1:5 [NRSV]

> **"** Every believer in this world
> must become a spark of light."
>
> Pope John XXIII

Focus for this Session

- We are called out of "night" into "day"
- Christ is the Light of the world
- Christians are called to live as children of the light

GATHER
Opening Prayer

Leader   Let us spend a few moments in quiet,
becoming more aware of God's presence ...
... God's presence in each one of us,
but especially in this community,
gathered in Jesus' name.
Pause for a few moments of quiet.
Then pray together:

Reader   God of Light,
you sent your Son among us
to lead all humanity
    from darkness into the light of faith.
May your Spirit open our minds
    and hearts to your Word today.
May your Word shed light
both on the ways we failed to respect
    your Covenant of love
and on how we ourselves
can be lights shining in the darkness.

All   **Amen**

Suggested Song
Holy Darkness

Living Our Faith

Share briefly your experience of putting into effect the action you chose after the last session.

BREAKING OPEN OUR STORY
Reflection

A few years ago I was giving a workshop in a local parish during Lent. The day included reflections on the themes relating to conversion, waking up from our sleep, and becoming light to the world. At some point during the gathering we pondered the words spoken by Saint Paul, "In Christ we live and move and have our being" (Acts 17:28).

All the participants were deeply touched by the notion that we are always in Christ, and that in him we live. Suddenly, the lights went out and the parish hall was plunged into darkness. People were frightened. Some began to caution others not to move in case they trip over something and fall. The parish sacristan, who was taking part in the workshop, started to give orders loudly: "Don't move, please. Remain calm!" No doubt concerned about people getting hurt in "his" parish, he seemed to want to take control of the situation. "There are flashlights in the kitchen," he said, "please stay in your places, I'll go get them." In the darkness I could hear whispers and murmurs of concern, fear, and nervous laughter.

No one suspected that while they were absorbed in the sharing, I had turned off the lights! After about six minutes of this chaos, I flipped the wall switch on and the hall was once again filled with light. Some observant participant noticed that I was standing next to the switch and, knowing my sense of humor, yelled, "You did it! You turned off the lights!" I waited until everyone calmed down and the sacristan returned from his attempt to make it to the kitchen, and then I confessed, "Yes, you're right. I turned the lights off."

Some laughed, although they really did not understand why I had played that trick on them. Others were rightfully upset with me and gave me all sorts of mean looks. After a minute or so, I asked them, "How many of you knew where the light switch was?" Those who belonged to that parish raised their hands. "Why didn't you try the light switch sooner?" I asked them. One of them honestly responded, "Because we were overcome by the darkness and couldn't think about anything else."

We spent the rest of the evening sharing on the theme of light and darkness. Although I had played a trick on them and apologized for it, the experience helped us see more clearly how difficult it is to switch on the Christ-life that is within us, when we allow the darkness to engulf us.

Invitation to Share

Take a few moments of silence to reflect on one of the following questions. Then share your reflections.

1. Share an experience when you were left in the dark: a moment of darkness for you personally, or for your family, or for your parish, or your community.

2. Share an experience of being helped, or helping someone else, overcome the darkness. Were you comforted or enlightenened in these moments by anything in Scripture?

BREAKING OPEN GOD'S STORY

The Word of God

Sometime before the meeting, the leader asks a member of the group to be prepared to proclaim the passage from the Gospel according to John.

John 3:1-21

"The light has come into the world."

Reader   *The Gospel of the Lord.*

All   **Praise to you, Lord Jesus Christ.**

Reflect

Moment of silent reflection

• What word, phrase, or image from the Scripture reading touched my heart or spoke to my life?

Invitation to Share

The leader invites those who so wish to echo a key word or phrase that touched them from the Scripture passage.

Reflection

"At night." It may sound like a matter of fact statement, but in reality John begins this passage in a highly symbolic way: Nicodemus, most likely a member of the Jewish council, the Sanhedrin, comes to see Jesus "at night".

Nicodemus not only greets Jesus as "Rabbi" (which means "teacher') but adds explicitly he recognizes him as a teacher "come from God." Nicodemus talks about Jesus' "signs" and shows how he interprets these as impossible "apart from the presence of God."

Jesus begins by recognizing what is valuable in Nicodemus' greeting, because it clearly shows Nicodemus is looking for the coming of the reign of God. A very good start! But is this "faith"? A question we can ask, not only about Nicodemus but about ourselves. In other words, is "looking for" the same as "seeing"?

Jesus says, "No one can see the kingdom of God without being born from above." Nicodemus takes this literally, which provides the springboard for Jesus to explain further. In what follows, Jesus' words are crammed with a whole series of contrasts, all designed to help Nicodemus—and us—enter into the mystery of the new life to which God calls us.

Nicodemus seems to want this rebirth but asks, "How can it happen?" Jesus gently reprimands him for not seeing that this is at the heart of the Jewish faith: after all, the Law (Torah) is praised in the psalms precisely because it is "a light for the eyes," bringing new

The use of opposites in the Gospel according to John

Another literary technique employed throughout the Gospel according to John is the use of dramatic contrasts. This means the "signs" this Gospel sets before us are accentuated, not just presenting them positively, but also by inviting us to consider their opposites.

We already saw in Session Three how water takes on a greater significance because it comes in response to thirst.

This Session, in this encounter between Jesus and Nicodemus, darkness heightens the strength and meaning of light.

The Gospel, though, goes further. It invites us to use the simple and dramatic contrast between dark and light to understand several other deeper, spiritual contrasts that all appear in this same Gospel passage:

being born	being born again
flesh	spirit
earthly things	heavenly things
death	eternal life
unbelief	belief
hating the light	coming to the light
condemnation	salvation
evil	truth

And all of this is set up from the very beginning because Nicodemus comes seeking:

enlightenment	"at night" …

life, wisdom, joy, richer than gold, sweeter than honey … (Psalm 19:7-10).

Then Jesus' explanation takes a profound turn: he himself is the source of this new life! This is the truth with which John's Gospel begins: that the Word is sent by God to be our light, a light that shines in the darkness, a light that the darkness cannot overpower (John 1:1-5, 9). Later in this same Gospel Jesus proclaims: "I am the light of the world. Whoever follows me will never walk in darkness but will have the light of life" (John 8:12). We are called out of darkness into light. This is exactly how the Bible opens (Genesis 1:1): darkness, the Spirit over the water, God's Word brings light!

The question Nicodemus asks, "How can this happen?" is, in fact, the fundamental question that Lent puts before us, and whose answer is celebrated by the liturgy of Holy Week. It happens through Christ, but in particular through Christ's Paschal Mystery, and by our sharing in this Mystery first through Baptism, and then through lifelong conversion. Jesus refers to an Old Testament episode that Nicodemus would know well: how the people of Israel in the desert were saved from death by looking upon the bronze serpent (see Numbers 21:4-9). In order to lift us up (to new life), Christ himself must first be "lifted up." Christ willingly endures death, the greatest of human darknesses, in order to bring us through to the light that no darkness can overpower. Rising from death, Christ calls everyone out of the darkness of unbelief to accept him, the Light. This was the meaning of his words to Nicodemus. Those who reject the light can be overcome by darkness, as were the people in the parish hall.

This is the Gospel passage that includes the well-known and much-quoted sentence: "For God so loved the world that he gave his only Son, so that everyone who believes in him may not perish but may have eternal life. Indeed, God did not send the Son into the world to condemn the world, but in order that the world might be saved through him" (John 3:16-17).

This is a concise and elegant summary of the heart of what we believe as Christians: first that Christ came into the world (Incarnation); secondly, Christ was sent by God to save us (Redemption). Above all, that both are done out of supreme love. It is important that we see both Incarnation and Redemption together, both as part of God's eternal plan of love for us that began by calling everything into the light of being (Creation).

Throughout this Season our focus has been conversion; today Jesus offers us the image of moving from darkness into light. It is a symbol of coming to faith in Christ, which we celebrate in our Baptism. Immediately after we are baptized, we (or our godparents on our behalf if we were too young) were entrusted with a candle, lit from the great Paschal Candle that symbolizes Christ, the light of the world. It was entrusted to us with these words: "... this light is entrusted to you to be kept burning brightly. You have been enlightened by Christ. You are to walk always as a child of the light. May you keep the flame of faith alive in your heart."

> ### God's thirst for us; our thirst for God
>
> "   The Paschal Candle should be ... of sufficiently large size that it may convey the truth that Christ is the light of the world. The Paschal Candle is the symbol of the light of Christ, rising in glory, scattering the darkness of our hearts and minds. Above all, the Paschal Candle should be a genuine candle, the pre-eminent symbol of the light of Christ."
>
> USCCB Committee on Divine Worship

This Season of Lent (and of ***ARISE***) is an opportunity to ask ourselves how brightly we have kept the flame of faith burning in our hearts. We celebrate this profound questioning in another sacrament, the Sacrament of Reconciliation, where we invite the light of Christ into whatever corners of our life we have allowed the darkness of sin to gather.

How did Nicodemus respond to what Jesus told him? In the short term, we do not know; the Gospel does not tell us. But we do know that precisely after Christ was "lifted up" on the cross, Nicodemus is there to anoint Jesus' body (see John 19:38-42). In so doing, he honors Jesus as "the Christ," "the anointed." This we hear in the closing words of the Passion proclaimed in the Good Friday liturgy.

Then on Holy Saturday night, during the Paschal Vigil, we will be asked to stand ("Arise"), and—holding candles lit from the Paschal Candle—to declare publicly our "conversion": to renounce the darkness that we want to leave behind; to reaffirm our promise to live as children of the light.

The moments in the liturgy are profound and communal expressions of our faith: but faith is about more than that. Faith is a loving response to God who not only gave us life but calls us in love to new life. The burning question is the one Nicodemus dares to ask: How will this happen? Lent is a God-given opportunity to think the question through. The real answer comes in the way we live the rest of our lives. In darkness? Or in light?

Invitation to Share

Take a few moments of silence to reflect on the following questions. Then share your reflections.

1. We are about half way through the season of Lent. How well am I using this time to look at my life, my attitudes? To let the light of Christ help me see things more clearly?

2. Share what you think are the spiritual darknesses that threaten our world today. Share, too, what we could be doing (personally and as a community) to combat this.

3. At our Baptism we were told "to walk as a child of the light," and "to keep the flame of faith burning in our hearts." Make the question of Nicodemus your own: how will this happen? What are some ways we can help to make this happen?

INVITATION TO ACT

Sharing and being together in a small Christian community fosters growth in our faith and in our spirituality. However, no communal sharing is complete without a serious commitment to putting our faith into practice.

In this session we have reflected on our call to live in the light of Christ and to move away from the darkness: to what kind of action does this inspire us?

Some Suggestions

1. Identify a situation in your family, workplace, parish, neighborhood that is "dimming" the light. Commit to a simple but concrete act that will bring light to that situation.

2. Take time at the end of each day to make an examen of consciousness (see sidebar.)

3. In the conversation with Nicodemus, Jesus talks about "seeing the kingdom of God." What can I do this week to make the kingdom of God more visible to those with whom I come into contact?

4. In the Gospel passage we hear Jesus warning against "loving darkness rather than light." Take time this week to prepare for the Sacrament of Reconciliation.

5. As part of your night prayer this week, light a candle, and pray:

> Christ, shed your light on my life.
> This evening/tonight I bring to you ...
> *(name a concern that darkened your day, or your relationship with someone).*
> Christ, be my light!

Examen of Consciousness

After quieting yourself and placing yourself in the presence of God...

1. Give thanks to God for today...

2. Ask for the grace to recognize and change your shortcomings of today...

3. Look back over your day being aware of your gratefulness for the day, "finding God in all things" in your day, and seeing how you responded to people, places, and things today...

4. Ask God for forgiveness for the times you have fallen short today and for help in understanding these times...

5. Make a plan for tomorrow and ask for God's help in living it out.

Adapted from the Spiritual Exercises *of St. Ignatius of Loyola*

Closing Prayer

Leader	Let us listen to the words of Christ.
Reader 1	Jesus says: "I am the light of the world. Whoever follows me will never walk in darkness, but will have the light of life."

John 8:12 [NRSV]

Pause

Reader 2	Jesus says: "Walk while you have the light so that the darkness may not overtake you. If you walk in the darkness, you do not know where you are going. While you have the light, believe in the light, so that you may become children of light."

John 12:35-36 [NRSV]

Pause

Leader	I invite you to present petitions, in a single word or a short phrase, asking the Father, through Christ, who was sent to be our Light, for the help and grace we need to walk as children of light.

To each petition, we respond:
Christ, be our light!

After the petitions, the following concluding prayer can be led by one person, or recited by all:

Lord Jesus,
you are the true light that enlightens all.
By the Spirit of truth,
free all who struggle under the yoke
of lies and deception.
Grant that we may enjoy your light
and inspire us to be fearless witnesses to the faith,
for you are Lord for ever and ever.
Amen.

Suggested Song
The Lord Is My Light

Looking Ahead

Prepare for the next faith-sharing meeting by reading over Session Five.

In particular:

• *Read the "Focus of this Session" (on page 57).*

• *Read the Scripture passage: **Jeremiah 31:31-34.**
It would help you set this passage in context if you were to read all of chapter 31.*

• *It may help to read the sidebar below.*

Jeremiah 31:31-34

The new covenant to be made with Israel is a common theme of the prophets, beginning with Hosea. According to Jeremiah, the qualities of the new covenant that make it different are:

a. It will not be broken, but will last forever;

b. Its law will be written in the heart, not merely on tablets of stone;

c. The knowledge of God will be so generally shown forth in the life of the people that it will no longer be necessary to put it into words of instruction.

New American Bible

Bound Together by a Promise

> *Do not despair, thinking that you cannot change yourself after so many years. Simply enter into the presence of Jesus as you are and ask him to give you a fearless heart where he can be with you. You cannot make yourself different; Jesus came to give you a new heart, a new spirit, a new mind, and a new body. Let him transform you by his love and so enable you to receive his affection in your whole being."*

From *Reaching Out: The Three Movements of Spirituality*
by Henri Nouwen

> *God does not want our deeds;
> God wants the love that prompts them."*

Saint Teresa of Avila

Focus for this Session

- The Covenant between God and God's people
- The Covenant is founded on love
- The Covenant is a two-way pledge of
  — faithfulness
  — mercy and forgiveness
- The New Covenant fulfilled in Christ

GATHER
Opening Prayer

Leader   Let us spend a few moments in quiet,
becoming more aware of God's presence ...
... God's presence in each one of us,
but especially in this community,
gathered in Jesus' name.

Pause for a few moments of quiet.
Then one member of the group reads the following
prayer:

God of mercy and forgiveness,
may the penance we live out this Lent
help us find new life in Christ.
May your Spirit strengthen us to live out
the covenant of love you entrust to us
in the person of Christ, your Son.
Inspire us by the love of Christ
and guide us by his example.
Grant this through Christ our Lord.

All   **Amen.**

Suggested Song
On Eagles' Wings

Living our Faith

Share briefly your experience of putting into effect the
action you chose after the last session.

BREAKING OPEN OUR STORY
Reflection

I still remember the profound impression made on
me the first time I read about the following advertisement that appeared in the classified columns of a
Madrid newspaper:

"Dear Paco,
Meet me in front of this newspaper's office
at noon on Saturday.
All is forgiven. I love you.
(Signed) Your father."

We can only guess at the story that led to this poignant advertisement. What led to their being estranged from one another? Was it something the son did or said? Was the offense real or imagined? We don't know.

We do, however, know the result: on Saturday, 800 Pacos showed up, each looking to welcome the love and forgiveness of their father.

There are bonds that all of us have experienced, between ourselves and our parents, or between ourselves as parents and our children. These are bonds that may be enshrined in law, but the law is an expression of something deeper. Most of us would say these are bonds that arise out of love, that they are written on hearts. And as long as they are ties of love, we do not find them a burden: being a parent or a partner in marriage can be tiring, exhausting physically and emotionally ... but it is in this that we find fulfillment, both our own fulfillment and yet a greater fulfillment in seeing the other flourish.

Love ties with bonds that can never be broken ... yet true love knows when to let go, because love can never constrain. Our children remain our children forever, and yet there comes the moment when we can no longer treat them as "children". One of the metaphors we use for this is to talk about "leaving the nest."

The Scripture scholar, Barnabas Ahern, describes an experience while visiting Petra, the ancient city in modern day Jordan:

"I shall never forget that day that I stood on the barren plain at Petra with its walls of blood-red rock. Glancing up, I saw a large bird soar from a mountain crag. Something dropped from its beak like a pellet of lead. In a moment the pellet unfolded, and I saw a little bird stretching its wings to fly.

Before long, however, the uprush of wind proved too strong and the little bird, once more a stone in the sky, began to drop. In an instant the other bird swooped down and caught it on her back to bear it aloft for a second trial.

This time, the young bird sustained itself in flight; but once more it crumpled before the wind and began to drop. But the ever-present mother saved it again for a third testing. As before, the pellet dropped, the wings opened, but this time the young bird flew off."

Some three months after they escaped slavery in Egypt, the people of Israel pitched camp facing a mountain called Sinai. Their leader, Moses climbed the mountain, where God gave him this message for the people: "You have seen what I did to the Egyptians, and how I bore you on eagles' wings, and brought you to myself. Now, therefore, if you obey my voice and keep my covenant, you shall be my treasured possession out of all peoples." (Exodus 19:4-5)

Invitation to Share

Take a few moments of silence to reflect on the following question. Then share your reflections.

1. Share what strikes you most about the story of Paco and his father.

FAITH

2. Look back on your life and share a moment when you felt you were "borne on eagles' wings."

BREAKING OPEN GOD'S STORY
The Word of God

Sometime before the meeting, the leader asks a member of the group to be prepared to proclaim the passage from the Prophet Jeremiah.

Jeremiah 31:31-34

I will make a new covenant ...
and remember their sin no more."

Reader   *The Word of the Lord.*

All   **Thanks be to God.**

Reflect

Moment of silent reflection

What word, phrase, or image from the Scripture reading touches my heart or speaks to my life?

Invitation to Share

The leader invites those who so wish to echo a key word or phrase that touched them from the Scripture passage.

REFLECTION

If we had to reduce the entire Bible to just one expression, it might be "covenant." We do that literally when we talk about the "Old Testament" and the "New Testament." The word "covenant" means a mutual agreement, that carries with it both privileges and obligations, both rights and responsibilities. It is a word that existed already before it was adopted in Scripture. Very often it was used to describe the agreement between a sovereign and his people; it could also refer to a peace treaty between tribes and nations; it was also a way that was used to describe what we would nowadays call a marriage contract.

The Bible presents the Covenant as an agreement that is offered by God to his people. In its simplest expression it is "I will be your God and you will be my people." What God asks is always a response to what God has already done.

The foundational experience for Israel is escaping from slavery (Exodus 14 and 15). Then, in the desert under the leadership of Moses, this Covenant comes to be expressed in what we now call the Ten Commandments. These do not begin with "You shall not ..." As we saw at the end of the first reflection, God begins by saying "I bore you on eagles' wings," and in particular, "I am the Lord God who brought you out of slavery"; only then are the ten key obligations laid out (see Exodus 20 and Deuteronomy 5).

At the heart of the obligations lay the experience of slavery, of being second-class people, on the fringes.

The people of God were expected to show the same loving kindness to others as God had shown them, particularly to "orphans," "widows," and "strangers."

A Covenant of Love

" Before God gave the commandments at Sinai, he entered into a covenant of love with the community of Israel (cf. Exodus 19:3-6). Once the covenant was established, God gave the people the Ten Commandments in order to teach them the way to live the covenant of love.

In Christ we have been called to a New Covenant and a New Law that fulfills and perfects the Old Law. We also are invited to experience God's love for us and to return that love to God and to our neighbor. Our love of neighbor includes our solidarity with the human community and a commitment to social justice for all."

United States Catholic Catechism for Adults,
page 325

As the People of God reflected on their experience through the eyes of faith, they looked back to the time before the giving of the Law on Mount Sinai. They saw "covenant" in the story of their ancestor Abraham (Genesis 15), and saw this renewed in his son Isaac (Genesis 26). Much later, confronted with pagan stories of the origins of humanity, the people of God would respond with their own stories of creation (Genesis 1:1—2:4) and the flood (Genesis 6:5—9:17) as expressions of God's "Covenant."

But a "covenant" is a mutual obligation, with responsibilities as well as rights, with obligations as well as privileges. When disaster strikes the people of Israel, Jerusalem and the Temple are destroyed, and many are deported to Babylon, the prophets yet again invoke the "Covenant"—but from the other side.

The reading we heard from Jeremiah is a classic example. Jeremiah looks back over the history of the people of God, and invites honest faith sharing. Is it right to think of this disaster as God breaking his side of the Covenant? Certainly not! But it had clearly been broken by the people, personally and as a community. Does the message of Jeremiah stop there? That the disaster and suffering of the people is no more than they deserve because they had not kept their side of the Covenant? Quite the contrary; at one of the lowest moments in the experience of the people of God, God promises a new Covenant. It is not that it will replace the old covenant, but it will enrich it, fulfill it. It will not be carved on tablets of stone, but written on their hearts. The first covenant was considered as something that had to be taught; the new covenant is something that will be experienced. Above all, the new Covenant is not one of retribution, but one of unconditional mercy and forgiveness. God says, "I will forgive their iniquity, and remember their sin no more."

The way in which the New Covenant is effected by God is founded on a twofold act of love. God takes on our human nature. What we call the Incarnation is the first step in the New Covenant, nothing less than an irrevocable commitment, not just to a people but to the whole human race. God does this, not despite our sins, but because we are sinful! This Covenant is so irrevocable that nothing can limit God's love for us. This unconditional love is expressed in the person of Jesus, and above all in his passion and death.

The Newness of the New Covenant

" The real mark of the New Covenant is this: in Jesus Christ God has bound himself to us human beings, has let himself be bound by us. The New Covenant no longer rests on the reciprocal keeping of the agreement: it is granted by God as grace that abides even in the face of our unfaithfulness. It is the expression of God's love, which will not allow itself to be defeated by our incapacity, but always remains well-disposed toward us, welcomes us again and again precisely because we are sinful, turns to us, sanctifies us, and loves us."

Joseph Ratzinger,
Introduction to Catholic Theology,
page 263

Through Jesus, God has established a bond with the human family:
"... a bond that can never be broken.
When we were lost
and could not find our way to God,
God loved us more than ever.
Jesus, God's Son, innocent and without sin,
gave himself into our hands
and was nailed to a cross.
Before he stretched out his arms
between heaven and earth
in the everlasting sign of the New Covenant,
he celebrated the Passover feast
with his disciples.
He took bread, gave thanks, broke the bread and
gave it saying,

This is my body ... given up for you.'
At the end of the meal,
knowing he was to reconcile all things to
himself
by the blood of the cross,
he took the cup, gave thanks, gave it to his
friends and said:
'This is the cup of my blood, the blood of the
new and everlasting covenant.
It will be shed for you and for all
for the forgiveness of sins.'"

*(see Eucharistic Prayer
for Masses of Reconciliation I).*

Jesus, the Son of God, became the Covenant and through the gift of the Holy Spirit carves this Covenant in our hearts forever. When we pray "Our Father," in saying "our" we recognize that we are a people bound together by the New Covenant that God has made with us through his Son in the Holy Spirit. We are the new people of God, called not to teach the ways of God, but to live the ways of God, to live the way of love. At the heart of the message of Christ is the command: "Love one another as I have loved you ...".

Lent is a time of grace and reconciliation. A time of conversion: of turning back to God, of responding to the Covenant. Meeting in our *ARISE* groups has helped us to reflect on it collectively. No matter how much others help us, ultimately we each have to make our own response:

"Dear Reader,
Meet me wherever, whenever you want.
All is forgiven. I love you.
(Signed) God."

Invitation to Share

Take a few moments of silence to reflect on the following questions. Then share your reflections.

1. What message do you believe God has written on all of our hearts?

   What special message do you believe God has written in your heart?

2. "I will remember their sins no more." What does this promise say to me about God?

3. In what ways will we live out the Covenant demands of forgiveness and mercy?

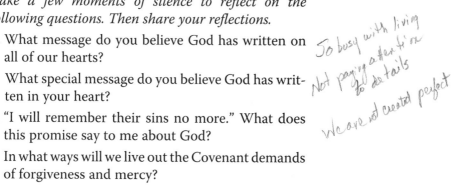

So busy with living
Not paying attention to details
We are not created perfect

INVITATION TO ACT

Sharing and being together in a small Christian community fosters growth in our faith and in our spirituality. But no communal sharing is complete without a serious commitment to putting our faith into practice.

In this session we have reflected on God's Covenant: "I will be your God, and you will be my people." This is both a privilege and responsibility. To what kind of action does being the people of the New Covenant inspire us?

Some Suggestions

1. Each day this week take time in prayer to thank God for the mercy and faithfulness he has shown to you (you might like to use the Covenant Litany from this session's closing prayer). Demonstrate this thankfulness by reaching out this week in mercy to those who need help or support in your community: for example, victims of fire, violence, or natural disaster, those who are hungry, or held in detention centers, etc.

2. Identify areas of your life where you have been less than responsive to God's love. If possible, do this in a guided way, for example, as part of a Lenten Retreat, or by taking part in a Penitential Service in your parish or deanery.

3. If you have not already done so, celebrate the Sacrament of Reconciliation as part of your preparation for Easter.

CLOSING PRAYER

Leader   Our God seeks out what is lost,
leads home the abandoned,
binds up what is broken,
and gives strength to the weak.
We turn in confidence
to the God of the Covenant of love,
and pray.

Response   **God of the Covenant, hear our prayer.**

You rescue us from slavery to sin.
Lead us to freedom in Christ.

Response   **God of the Covenant, hear our prayer.**

Make us a living sign of your love for all to see.

Response   **God of the Covenant, hear our prayer.**

May we grow in your peace,
and seek to spread it throughout the world.

Response   **God of the Covenant, hear our prayer.**

In love you forgive us our sins;
may it teach us to love others,
and to forgive their sins against us.

Response   **God of the Covenant, hear our prayer.**

Look on our weakness;
do not be angry and condemn,
but in your love cleanse, guide, and save us.

Response   **God of the Covenant, hear our prayer.**

In your mercy free us from the past
and enable us to begin a new life.

Response   **God of the Covenant, hear our prayer.**

By your redeeming love
overcome our sinfulness
and the harm it has brought us.

Response **God of the Covenant, hear our prayer.**

Cleanse and renew your Church, Lord;
make it grow in strength as a witness to your
Covenant of love.

Response **God of the Covenant, hear our prayer.**

Touch the hearts of those who have abandoned you
because of sin and scandal;
call them back to you
and keep them faithful in your love.

Response **God of the Covenant, hear our prayer.**

You sent your Son to us
as the new and eternal Covenant.
You call us to arise together in Christ.
May we never lose the gifts
you have given us in Christ.

Response **God of the Covenant, hear our prayer.**

May we be faithful to the Covenant of love
you have written on our hearts.

Response **God of the Covenant, hear our prayer.**

All pray the final blessing together

**May the Father bless us,
for we are his children, born to eternal life.
May the Son show us his saving power,
for he died and rose for us.
May the Spirit who dwells in our hearts
give us his gift of holiness
and lead us by the right path.**

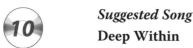

Suggested Song
Deep Within

Sign of Peace

Leader   May the peace of the Lord be always with us.
Let us offer each other a sign of peace.

Looking Ahead

Prepare for the next faith-sharing meeting by reading over Session Six.

In particular:

• *read the "Focus of this Session" (on page 69).*

• *read the Scripture passage: Philippians 2:6-11. It would help to set this passage in context if you were to read the first five verses of the chapter.*

Into Holy Week with Christ

> " *Make ready for the Christ, Whose smile like lightning*
> *Sets free the song of everlasting glory,*
> *That now sleeps, in your paper flesh, like dynamite."*
>
> From the poem "The Victory" by Thomas Merton
> in the book of poems *A Man in the Divided Sea*

> " *Father, all powerful and ever-living God,*
> *in Christ you have renewed all things*
> *and you have given us a share in his riches.*
> *Though his nature was divine,*
> *he stripped himself of glory*
> *and by shedding his blood on the cross*
> *he brought peace to the world.*
> *Therefore he was exalted above all creation*
> *and became the source of eternal life*
> *to all who serve him."*
>
> From the Preface for Weekdays I, *Roman Missal*

Focus for this Session

- Sharing in the great "conversion" of death into life
- Celebrating and making present the "triumph" of the cross
    — in liturgy
    — in life
- Sharing in the "Paschal Mystery"
- The "Paschal Mystery" as the foundation of our faith, our hope, and our love

GATHER

Opening Prayer

Set up a crucifix or an icon, or at least a picture of the Cross, if possible one that shows Christ in triumph (for example, Christ as High Priest on the Cross).

Leader Let us spend a few moments in quiet,
becoming more aware of God's presence ...
... God's presence in each one of us,
but especially in this community,
gathered in Jesus' name.

Pause for a few moments of quiet.

Suggested Song
Unless a Grain of Wheat

Leader We should glory in the cross
of our Lord Jesus Christ,

All **for he is our salvation.**

Leader We should glory in the cross
of our Lord Jesus Christ,

All **for he is our life.**

Leader We should glory in the cross
of our Lord Jesus Christ,

All **for he is our resurrection.**

Leader We should glory in the cross
of our Lord Jesus Christ,

All **for through him we are saved and made free.**

(Based on Galatians 6:14)

Living Our Faith

Share briefly your experience of putting into effect the action you chose after the last session.

BREAKING OPEN OUR STORY
Reflection

Throughout this second Season of **ARISE**, as we have journeyed through Lent, our central theme has been "conversion." A word that basically means "turn-around."

Our century was one of immense "turnarounds," both high points and utterly low points. The fall of the Berlin Wall and what it stood for was a high point for more than those who happened to live in Berlin. How many of us still remember exactly where we were when we heard the news about the planes flying into the Twin Towers?

As part of my chaplaincy work in a Catholic high school in France, I twice took groups of senior students to Auschwitz. A journey for which we tried to prepare the students—but can you ever be prepared for the immensity that awaits you there?

We invited Francine Christophe, a camp survivor, to share her story. Although Francine was never an inmate at the Auschwitz death camp, she was interned at several concentration camps, including the notorious Bergen-Belsen.

She recounted for us how, as a young girl, life changed, simply because she was Jewish. Jews needed a permit for a radio, then later they were not allowed radios at all. Shops were open to Jews only at certain limited times. She remembers a children's play park marked "No entry for dogs and Jews."

When Francine and her mother attempted to get to the free zone in France, they were discovered

> ## I Didn't Speak Up
>
> First they came for the Communists,
>   and I didn't speak up,
>   because I wasn't a Communist.
> Then they came for the Jews,
>   and I didn't speak up,
>   because I wasn't a Jew.
> Then they came for the Catholics,
>   and I didn't speak up,
>   because I was a Protestant.
> Then they came for me,
>   and by that time
>   there was no one left
>   to speak up for me.
>
> Rev. Martin Niemoller, 1945

(perhaps betrayed), arrested, and interned. The calculated psychological stripping of these people of their dignity as citizens now went a step further: an attempt to strip them of their very humanity. The personal belongings and tons of human hair now heaped in show cases at Auschwitz bear awful testimony to this designed descent into hell.

Francine remembers with sadness, that for many it worked; how some internees became like animals, others became empty shells. I have looked into many pairs of eyes, caught for history in the Auschwitz identity photos. In too many of those eyes, the light has long since been extinguished; I check the dates and note that within days, weeks of the photo, they would be dead. And yet there are other photos, their faces as Isaiah would have said "set like flint," in which you can read determination, fire, spirit ...

What was remarkable about Francine's way of telling her story were the many moments of simple but profound expressions of humanity.

How the first day she had to wear her yellow star, the headmistress—in front of the whole class— simply took her in her arms and hugged her. It could have cost her job, and worse.

How Jews could only travel in the last carriage on the Paris subway, and had to stand. Francine remembers how many ordinary people opted to board that carriage and stand. A small but eloquent symbol of solidarity.

How at one concentration camp a guard (in civilian life, a customs officer) would pick an apple fallen from the trees around the camp and discretely pass it to her through the wires.

In a world designed to inspire despair, these represented tiny but no less real glimmers of hope.

The People of God have long since reflected on the basic human experience of humiliation, slavery, "man's inhumanity to man" as the Scottish poet Burns put it. Reading that experience through the eyes of faith is the foundation for two central truths, which belong inextricably together:

humanity is *in need* of redemption;
humanity is *capable* of redemption.

Put simply: on our own, we are lost; but we are never on our own, for the God who created us can recreate us. More, God so longs to recreate us that he is with us at our lowest, so as to bring us to the highest.

Invitation to Share

Take a few moments of silence to reflect on one of the following questions. Then share your reflections.

1. Share briefly an event (personal or public) that you felt brought you low, or that saddened you deeply. Share something that someone else did or said that lifted you out of a particularly low moment.

2. Do you find it easier to be aware of the presence of God, or to turn to God in prayer, in "low" moments, or in "high" moments?

BREAKING OPEN GOD'S STORY
The Word of God

Sometime before the meeting, the leader asks a member of the group to be prepared to proclaim the passage from St. Paul's Letter to the Philippians.

Philippians 2:6-11
Christ humbled himself, but God raised him high

> Reader   *This is the Word of the Lord.*
>
> **All**   **Thanks be to God**

Reflection

Moment of silent reflection

• What word, phrase, or image from the Scripture reading touches my heart or speaks to my life?

Invitation to Share

The leader invites those who so wish to echo a key word or phrase that touched them from the Scripture passage.

Reflection

We are about to enter a week that celebrates a remarkable "turnaround," and the way the liturgy invites us into this week is with a remarkable text, the one we just heard proclaimed from Paul's Letter to the Philippians.

One of the most profound ways we express our faith is through the liturgy, and in particular through the hymns we sing. When Paul writes to the Christians at Philippi and wants to invite them to welcome Christ as the key to life and death, he embeds into his message what was clearly a hymn already being used by Christians. We take it on our lips today, at the end of a chain of faith sharing that stretches back some 1,950 years, proclaiming now, as did the first generation after the Resurrection, the salvation that God brought about for us in Christ.

In most Bibles this text is set out in sense lines, carefully arranged to respect the poetry of the original. We, too, should respect this, because in fact the very structure of the passage helps convey the central message. That central message is what we refer to as "the Paschal Mystery." The word "paschal" is derived from the Greek word meaning "pass over." At its very heart it is less about events and more about movement: it is about both "from ..." and "to ...": from slavery to freedom, from death to life.

The Paschal Mystery

" When we speak of the Paschal Mystery, we refer to Christ's death and Resurrection as one inseparable event. It is a mystery because it is a visible sign of an invisible act of God. It is paschal because it is Christ's passing through death into new life. For us it means we can now die to sin and its domination of our lives, and we pass over into divine life already here on earth and more completely in heaven."

United States Catholic Catechism for Adults,
page 93

The song has two great movements. It begins with the words "Jesus Christ" who is honored by the song as being God. Then there is the first movement, a great swoop downwards: Jesus sets aside his divinity, "humbling" himself to take our humanity, to accept that most basic of all human characteristics:

death. Paul himself adds an extra line to the hymn at this point: Jesus accepts not just death but "death on a cross."

Then the great swoop upwards of the song begins. Precisely because of this total acceptance by Jesus (expressed in the song as "obedience") God raises him on high—and with Christ and in Christ, all of humanity. The turning point is the line "even death on a cross."

"Death on a cross." A line that Paul adds not just to the center of the hymn, but to the center of his life! In all of his preaching and teaching, Paul invites us to do the same: to recognize the significance of this once and for all event. Christ's death is the greatest of turning points. It is the turning point for faith, but also for hope, and for love.

To the eyes of faith the cross represents not disgrace, but triumph. It is the triumph of love. The cross tells us how much God loves us. It tells us that there is a love in this world stronger than death, stronger than our weaknesses and sins. It is in faith that we dare to say, as we did in our opening prayer that we should "glory in the cross of our Lord Jesus Christ, for he is our salvation, our life, and our resurrection; through him we are saved and made free" (Galatians 6:14).

The cross is not only the sign of God's love. It makes us free to love as Christ loves us. This is why the cross is a sign of hope. There is hope in the cross, not because it means an end to suffering, but because it gives meaning to suffering: suffering assumed in the name of love, truth, justice—each are triumphs of love against hate, lies, injustice. On the night before he died, Jesus offers these words of hope to the apostles with a simple but profoundly human comparison: "When a woman is in labor, she has pain, because her hour has come. But when her child is born, she no longer remembers the anguish because of the joy of having brought a human being into the world" (John 16:21).

How does this relate to our first reflection? The memory of the death camps haunt humanity, because it reminds us of what we are capable. The way Jesus accepts suffering and death proves what humanity is capable of in exactly the opposite sense. As Pope Benedict, who lived through the horrors perpetrated in the name of his nation, said in his first homily as Pope: "It is not power, but love that redeems us! ... God, who became a lamb, tells us that the world is saved by the Crucified One, not by those who crucified him."

The whole purpose of Holy Week is to proclaim exactly this salvation. This is why we celebrate Holy Week—especially the Triduum of Holy Thursday, Good Friday, and the Easter Vigil.

The true measure of humanity

" The true measure of humanity is essentially determined in relationship to suffering and to the sufferer. This holds true for both the individual and for society.... The capacity to accept suffering for the sake of goodness, truth and justice is an essential criterion of humanity.

To suffer with the other and for others; to suffer for the sake of truth and justice; to suffer out of love and in order to become a person who truly loves—these are the fundamental elements of humanity, and to abandon them would destroy man himself.... Let us say it once again: the capacity to suffer for the sake of the truth is the measure of humanity. This capacity to suffer depends on the type and extent of hope that we bear within us and build upon."

Pope Benedict XVI
Spes salvi (Encyclical on Christian Hope), 38-39

The liturgies we are about to celebrate are not just commemorations of historical events. They make that once and for all supreme act of love real and present here and now. They pull us into that great movement we call the "Paschal Mystery." In these celebrations we accept to go down into the tomb with Jesus so that we can arise together in Christ.

What we have to celebrate is so big that the Church extends it for 50 days; the whole of the Season of Easter up to Pentecost! But just as Easter cannot be contained in one liturgical moment or day, so too the triumph that it brings for all people needs to be spread.

However, the hymn from Philippians gives us not just words to be sung during a liturgy. The faith these words express implies a different view of our humanity, and of how we treat each other, and the world God has entrusted to us. We are called not just to celebrate the sacraments, but to be sacraments—living signs of the love of God made real in Christ.

The fullness of Christ's humanity was proved by the cross. Does the fullness of our humanity not demand that we work to bring all those who are still living under the shadow of the tree of defeat and death into the light of the tree of life? Augustine says "We are an Easter people, and 'Alleluia!' is our song"—a song that remains incomplete until all have been brought into it. The call to arise in Christ is one we must not only answer ourselves, but make resonate throughout our communities.

Invitation to Share

Take a few moments of silence to reflect on one of the following questions. Then share your reflections.

1. Share what you strikes you most in the way Jesus approaches his passion and death. What could you do to emulate that?

2. If we really believe in a crucified Christ, who is risen from the dead, what difference should it make to the way we hope? What difference should it make to the way we love?

3. "It is not power that redeems us, but love!" Is ours a culture built on love … or on power? How will I, or we as a group, promote a culture built on love?

INVITATION TO ACT

Sharing and being together in a small Christian community fosters growth in our faith and in our spirituality. However, no communal sharing is complete without a serious commitment to putting our faith into practice.

In this session we have reflected on the Paschal Mystery: to what kind of action does this inspire us, both in the liturgies of Holy Week, and in life?

Some Suggestions

1. Commit to taking part in all three days of the Triduum: the Holy Thursday evening Mass, the Good Friday liturgy, and the Easter Vigil.

Gather as a faith-sharing group for an informal celebration of Easter (a picnic together, or potluck supper, with our families).

2. "The true test of our humanity is how we deal with suffering." Commit to an action this week, either individually or as a group, against torture, slavery, or injustice.

3. Set aside a moment to read Philippians 2:6-11 slowly and prayerfully. Take time to enjoy the way the text is built; perhaps write out the text, in two columns (verses 6-8, then verses 9-11). But remember this structure was meant to enhance the message, not distract from it. Pray in thanksgiving for the gift of the mystery of the Incarnation and the mystery of Redemption.

Philippians 2:6-11

The Church offers this text in the liturgy, not just as a reading to be proclaimed (on Passion Sunday and on the Feast of the Triumph of the Cross), but also as an acclamation and so to be sung.

In fact, the Church proposes that any proclamation of the Passion from the Gospels be prepared by singing this ancient hymn: verses 8-9 on Passion Sunday before the Passion according to Matthew, Mark, or Luke (depending on the year); and again on Good Friday before the proclamation of the Passion according to John.

4. The great call of Holy Week is to arise together in Christ. Share with family and friends your experience of these six weeks of Season Two of **ARISE**. Invite a friend, neighbor, or family member to join your **ARISE** group for Season Three (Fall).

Closing Prayer

Leader   The Father of mercies
has given us an example of unselfish love
in the suffering of his only Son.
Through our service of God and neighbor
may we receive God's countless blessings.

All   **Amen.**

Leader   We believe that by his dying
Christ destroyed death for ever.
May he give us everlasting life.

All   **Amen.**

Leader   Christ Jesus humbled himself for our sake.
May we follow his example
and share in his resurrection.

All   **Amen.**

*Adapted from the solemn blessing over the people
for Passion Sunday,* Roman Missal

Leader   God our Father,
by the paschal mystery of Christ your Son
you conquered the power of death
and opened for us the way to eternal life.
Let our celebration of Holy Week
raise us up and renew our lives
by the Spirit that is within us.
Grant this through Jesus Christ our Lord.

All   **Amen.**

Adapted from the Opening Prayer for Easter Sunday,
Roman Missal

Concluding Song

Suggested Song
Jesus the Lord

Music Resources
Alphabetical Index of Suggested Songs
(by first line and/or title)

As the Deer Longs (Psalm 42, 43)
Words, based on Psalm 42:2-4, 8, Psalm
43:3-4, and music: Bob Hurd
© 1988 OCP Publications

Change Our Hearts
Words and music: Rory Cooney
©1984, 1994 OCP Publications

Create in Me (Psalm 51)
Words, based on Psalm 51, and music:
Bob Hurd
© 1986 OCP Publications

Deep Within
Words, based on Jeremiah 31:33, Ezekiel
36:26, Joel 2:12, and music: David Haas
© 1987 GIA Publications, Inc.

Eye Has Not Seen
Words, based on 1 Corinthians 2:9-10,
and music: Marty Haugen
© 1982 GIA Publications, Inc.

Holy Darkness
Words, inspired by St. John of the Cross,
Daniel L. Schutte
Music: Daniel L. Schutte
© 1988, 1989, 1992, Daniel L. Schutte
Published by OCP Publications

Jesus the Lord
Words, based on the Jesus Prayer, Acts
17:28, Philippians 2:5-11, and music:
Roc O'Connor S.J.
© 1981 Roc O'Connor S.J. and OCP
Publications

On Eagle's Wings
Words, based on Psalm 91, and music:
Michael Joncas
© 1973, 2003 OCP Publications

The Lord is My Light
Words, based on Psalm 18, and Music:
John B. Foley, S.J© 1976 John B. Foley, S.J.
and OCP Publications

The Water I Shall Give
Words, based on John 5:4-42, Romans
5:5, Psalm 95:8, and music: Bob Hurd
© 2002 OCP Publications

Unless a Grain of Wheat
Words, based on John 12:24, and music:
Bernadette Farrell
© 1983 Bernadette Farrell
Published by OCP Publications

Who Calls You by Name
Words and Music: David Haas
© 1988 GIA Publications, Inc.

**You who dwell in the shelter of the
Lord**
See **On Eagle's Wings**

All of the songs listed above are on the *Change Our Hearts* CD, one sample copy of which is included in the *ARISE Parish Kit*. For further information, including how to order additional copies, see page 84.

Most of the songs suggested for the sessions can be found in the standard hymnals or parish worship aids. Should you want to get in touch with any of the publishers of the songs suggested (for example, to obtain printed copies of the music scores, or to purchase downloadable PDF, TIFF, or MP3 files, or to ask for permission to reprint copyright words), here are their contact details.

GIA Publications, Inc.
7404 South Mason Avenue
Chicago, IL 60638
Phone: 800-442-1358 or
              708-496-3800
Fax: 708-496-3828
Website: www.giamusic.com
Email: custserv@giamusic.com
For downloadable copies (as PDF or TIFF files, with preview and listen options): www.hymnprint.net

Oregon Catholic Press Publications (OCP)
5536 NE Hassalo
Portland, OR 97213
Phone: 800-LITURGY (548-8749)
Fax: 800-4-OCP-FAX (462-7329)
Website: www.ocp.org
Email: liturgy@ocp.org
Permissions processed through www.LicenSingonline.org
For downloadable copies in PDF and GIF format: www.printandpraise.com

ARISE Resources

The five Seasons of faith sharing in small Christian communities are central to the *ARISE Together in Christ* process.

For each Season, RENEW International offers a faith-sharing book, a CD with the songs suggested in the faith-sharing book, and a Seasonal Supplement to the *ARISE Liturgy Handbook*, offering pastoral notes and practical suggestions on how to link the process with the Sunday celebration of the Eucharist.

The five Seasons are:

Season One	**Encountering Christ Today**
Season Two	**Change Our Hearts**
Season Three	**In the Footsteps of Christ**
Season Four	**New Heart, New Spirit**
Season Five	**We Are the Good News**

To guide the Parish Team in their implementation of the *ARISE* process, we provide the *ARISE Parish Team Handbook*. This has been designed as a ring binder with two mains sections and an appendix of photocopiable handouts; as the process develops, additional material will be offered which can be added to the Handbook.

In addition, there are several general resources designed to foster the fruitful implementation of *ARISE*, and indeed, any faith-sharing process:

SOWING SEEDS Essentials for Small Community Leaders
Offers a comprehensive collection of pastoral insights and practical suggestions to help small community leaders guide their groups in a way that nourishes spiritual growth. Culled from RENEW International's three decades of experience in pioneering and promoting small Christian communities, this book overflows with simple but effective ideas and strategies that will enhance the way these groups reflect on and respond to the Gospel.

Gleanings: A Personal Prayer Journal
A valuable tool for both avid and occasional journal writers. Each of the handsomely decorated pages offers a spiritual quotation or musing that can inspire the user to prayerfully reflect on his or her relationship with God. The comfortably-sized format is conducive to many different methods of journaling: writing, poetry, or even sketching. An excellent companion for your personal faith journey, *Gleanings,* will help you tap into the richness of God's wisdom within you.

The **ARISE** Parish Kit contains one copy of each of the resources mentioned above, together with one copy of *PRAYER TIME Faith-Sharing Reflections on the Sunday Gospels* for each of Sunday cycles of readings (A, B, and C). A fuller description of this resource can be found on page 85.

The above resources can be found on the **ARISE** member pages of our website: www.renewintl.org/ARISEservices
You can also use our toll free order line: 1-888-433-3221.

The printed resources presented here are complemented by a range of web resources, all designed to help participants in the **ARISE** process make the most of this opportunity for pastoral and spiritual renewal in small communities and as a parish and diocesan community. Members can access these at: www.renewintl.org/ARISEservices

- *PRAYERTIME Cycle A, B, C:*
  Faith-Sharing Reflections on the Sunday Gospels

This faith-sharing resource that responds to the U.S. Bishops' suggestion for adult faith formation that "every parish meeting can begin with the reading of the upcoming Sunday's Gospel, followed by a time of reflection and faith sharing."

Using the Sunday Gospels as focus, *PRAYERTIME* proposes meaningful reflections, focused faith-sharing questions, related questions for consideration, and prayers as a source of spiritual nourishment, renewal, and inspiration.

Each book offers gentle but insightful reflections that help the Gospel come alive. Written in an easy-to-read style that leads to profound questions about faith, each session sheds light on everyday life and should bear fruit in realistic action.

It is recommended *PRAYERTIME* be used by groups between seasons of **ARISE**, as well as at pastoral council and parish staff meetings, and at the beginning of other parish group meetings. The themes for reflection have been designed so that they can also be used personally, and in groups.

- The **IMPACT** Series

The **IMPACT** Series aims to connect faith to a wide range of human concerns and pastoral issues, in a way that leads participants not only to prayerful reflection and fruitful sharing, but also to concrete actions that influence attitudes and behaviors.

Experience shows that such issues are seldom addressed without a certain amount of challenge, guidance, and assistance. The **IMPACT** Series is designed to meet this need and help small Christian communities fulfill their potential as workers for the kingdom, ushering in God's reign on earth.

Each book proposes a set of Sessions, so that across a period of several weeks the participants have time to observe and bring the fruit of these observations to their sharing; to measure these against the gospel, to reflect on how the gospel calls them to respond; and to commit themselves to concrete actions both as individuals and as a group. The participants are invited to use the time between the faith-sharing sessions for putting these commitments into action.

The **IMPACT** Series is divided into four categories of human and spiritual concerns:

> Sacramental Pathways
> Faith in Daily Life
> Spiritual Awakenings
> Discipleship in Action.

For more information about these, and many other resources, or to order, please consult our secure online bookstore:
www.renewintl.org/store
or use our toll free order line: 1-888-433-3221

Notes

Notes

Books: The Reader
        The Shack

A Time To:
    Listen
    Be fair
    Help others
    Pray
    Share
    Forgive